*Women Priests: The First*

# Women Priests

## The First Years

Edited by HILARY WAKEMAN

DARTON·LONGMAN+TODD

First published in 1996 by
Darton, Longman and Todd Ltd
1 Spencer Court
140–142 Wandsworth High Street
London SW18 4JJ

This collection © 1996 Hilary Wakeman

ISBN 0–232–52151–4

A catalogue record for this book is available
from the British Library

Acknowledgement:
Extract from 'Lord of the Years' by Timothy Dudley-Smith
is used by kind permission of the author.

Phototypeset by Intype London Ltd, London
Printed and bound in Great Britain
by Redwood Books, Trowbridge, Wilts

# Contents

|   |                                                                                           |     |
|---|-------------------------------------------------------------------------------------------|-----|
|   | *Notes on contributors*                                                                   | vii |
| 1 | What difference is women's priesthood making in the pews?<br>HILARY WAKEMAN                | 1   |
| 2 | What difference is women's priesthood making to women?<br>PAMELA FAWCETT                   | 27  |
| 3 | What is priesthood?<br>RUTH WINTLE                                                         | 43  |
| 4 | Recovering from gender stereotypes: codeines and kite<br>MARY ROBINS                       | 59  |
| 5 | A different way of working: what women bring to collaborative ministry<br>PENNY MARTIN     | 76  |
| 6 | Being realistic about feminism<br>BARBARA BAISLEY                                          | 97  |
| 7 | From expectations to realities: and the future<br>PATIENCE PURCHAS                         | 117 |
| 8 | What difference is women's priesthood making to the Church of England?<br>JUDITH ROSE      | 136 |

# Notes on contributors

The Revd **Barbara Baisley** is Advisor for Women's Ministry in the Diocese of Coventry, as well as being involved in vocations work and clergy training. She is married to a parish priest and is a member of General Synod.

The Revd Canon **Pamela Fawcett** is the Bishop of Norwich's Consultant for Women's Ministry, and Assistant Diocesan Director of Ordinands. She is a non-stipendiary priest in a rural team ministry.

The Revd **Penny Martin** was born in Wales and brought up in South London. She is about to become vicar of a three-parish benefice in Durham. She is married to a Professor of Theoretical Physics; they have three children.

The Revd **Patience Purchas** is the Bishop of St Albans' officer for women's and non-stipendiary ministry. She has written two devotional books, and has presented a Sunday morning programme on Chiltern Radio for four years. She is married to a parish priest and mother of two grown-up daughters.

The Revd **Mary Robins** is a priest at St James's, Piccadilly, and also in St Albans Diocese. She works in general ministry, spiritual guidance, adult education, and creating liturgies. Her particular concern is connecting sexuality and spirituality.

The Venerable **Judith Rose** is Archdeacon of Tonbridge, and Associate Diocesan Director of Ordinands. She has been in stipendiary ministry since 1966, was Chaplain to the Bishop of Rochester from 1990–95, and has been a member of the General Synod from 1975–81 and from 1987 onwards.

The Revd Canon **Hilary Wakeman** is the vicar of St George Colegate, Norwich and was a member of the General Synod from 1990–95.

The Revd Canon **Ruth Wintle** is Advisor for Women's Ministry in Worcester Diocese. Since 1967 her work has included being a student advisor in Oxford, Old Testament Tutor at Cranmer Hall, an ACCM Selection Secretary, and Diocesan Director of Ordinands. She was a member of General Synod 1990–95 and during that time was also a member of the Crown Appointments Commission.

# 1 What difference is women's priesthood making in the pews?

HILARY WAKEMAN

Shortly before his retirement, Archbishop John Habgood stated that although he unquestionably favoured the ordination of women, he could have wished it had taken longer. Many in the Church of England were distressed or irritated that he should say that when he did. The issue had seemed finally to be settling down. Arrangements for those opposed to women priests were thought to be working reasonably well, and the church appeared at last to be turning its eyes away from its own navel to the more vital concerns of the world around it.

However, behind the Archbishop's statement was no doubt his awareness of some painful pastoral situations. For this chapter I have tried to gauge the opinions and feelings of ordinary church-goers about the changes being brought about by the full priestly ministry of women in the church. I have talked with groups of people in urban and in rural parishes, in evangelical parishes and in those on the catholic wing; to those with experience of the ministry of women priests and those with none. And I have canvassed letters and telephone calls on the subject.

Contentment is not vociferous. The majority of people in the congregations of the Church of England are clearly either very pleased to have women priests, or have taken it in their stride, wondering what all the fuss was about.

© 1996 Hilary Wakeman

It is the opinions of those people who remain most implacably opposed to the whole concept that come across most strongly. Many of them are in real pain. The group who make the next strongest impression are those who are having serious difficulty in reconciling what their hearts are saying with what their heads are saying, and are distressed by the disparity.

In some areas I was told that one or two people had declined to meet with me, afraid that they might say things they would afterwards regret. This is understandable, but sad. Women priests now exist. The argument is over. Now we have to find out how, together, we may keep the church on the road to the kingdom of God.

'Now the human race isn't just male,' said a middle-aged man in a group of rural parishes. 'Now the priest, at the eucharist, is for all of us.' In the same group someone said: 'At the first service of [the new woman priest] I was apprehensive. Yet as soon as it happened my wife said it was like someone opened a door and put a new world on her God.'

Elsewhere, in an urban parish, a man not in the forefront of radical change — he is a devout upholder of the Prayer Book services — writes: 'The ministry has definitely been enriched ... I feel guilty that for so many years I have never seriously considered how much the church could be losing by restricting women's ministry. Now I know.'

It was no use pretending, in those days and years of debate before the momentous decision of General Synod in 1992, that nothing would change. It may have been tempting to say that nothing would be altered, in order to deflect people's fears of unfaceable horrors to come ('It'll be lay presidency at the eucharist before we know it'; 'They'll be ordaining practising homosexuals next'; 'We'll all have to call God "Mother" '). Yet none of us could do more than guess what the effect on the church would be. Now we begin to know.

The arguments that threatened to tear the church apart had to do with scripture, theology, doctrine, history and tradition, and what the Holy Spirit might be saying to the church. To what extent any of these, for or against women's ordination, were rationalizations of intuition, misogyny or gut feelings it was not proper to enquire. The same subconscious elements could be suspected in ordinary church-goers lacking the benefit or handicap of a theological education, or experience of synodical government (the confrontational way the Church of England governs itself). Yet those church-goers, if their opinions rested on anything other than 'plain common sense', usually mentioned only scripture or tradition. These grounds are still basic where there are objections to what the church has done. But there seemed no point in rehearsing them all again, and so in the groups I talked with, we tried to keep the emphasis on what is new.

An experience of wholeness in the church is something that was expected by supporters of the new legislation. They have not been disappointed. Men and women have been deeply moved by the simple sight of a woman standing at the altar, saying words so long forbidden to anyone born female. 'Now I feel there is a God who is represented by a whole human being,' was how one man put it. But the new wholeness of the church goes beyond gender complementarity. The church has grown, said a parishioner with long experience of the ministry of women: it has had to look at itself, it has had to become more tolerant, to do more consulting, and to do more teaching. The church, she believes, has been enlarged.

Women priests have brought 'a new, vibrant dimension to the C of E that we all love so well', wrote a man who had survived not only his clergy father's disapproval of women's ordination but also the trauma of not having his own vocation to the priesthood affirmed by the church. Such generosity of spirit makes it unsurprising that, as he says, he looks forward to the future.

Another expected result is that many women feel affirmed in the church by the arrival of women as priests: at least in theory. In practice, the phenomenon needs to be a local reality for such affirmation to be fully felt. In many churches with women as curates or as vicars or rectors there has been a new unleashing of gifts. This was the experience of a large Midlands parish which at one point had two women priests, as well as a woman parish worker and three women readers. 'Having women in ministry within the parish has enabled other women to affirm themselves,' one of the readers said. 'They feel able to take on roles which perhaps are more often associated with men: churchwarden, for example.' From a church in an industrial city another woman says similarly: 'One effect of [the new woman priest's] presence is the greater readiness of women churchgoers to take a prominent part in parish life.' But the affirmation extends beyond the functional. 'Seeing a woman at the altar celebrating the eucharist . . . women no longer feel cut off from "the holy bits", and have begun to find their voice.'

There were many references to the special gifts that women have for ministry. A man who twenty years ago was strongly opposed to women priests came to think that women's 'tremendous sensitivity' enables them to enter into situations difficult for most men. Another said that women are used to talking to each other about their problems, but that men find it hard – and almost impossible with another man. Women's gentleness in bereavement work was often mentioned. The way that a woman priest conducted a funeral was cited by one woman as an example of how the church was being changed.

My first thought was, 'It's no different'. It was good, and rich. But then – something she brought to it – the understanding that belongs to women – I enjoyed that service. I felt very comfortable and happy. Yes, I think women will give a different feeling to the church.

Another woman, previously opposed, was converted by hearing a woman preach in a cathedral. 'She was the most sincere person I had ever heard.' Again and again it was the encounter with individual women that had convinced people of the rightness of their priesthood. The man whose clergyman father had disagreed intensely with women's ordination says now of a local priest:

> She is forthright, humbly honest, an excellent organiser, has a beautiful singing voice and her sermons are instructive and a joy to listen to. Although she is totally unaware of it, she has convinced me that the ordination of women was correct and possibly long overdue.

Many of the problems in the church are the result of male dominance, another man thought. He believes that women are better listeners, more intuitive, and better able to engage in dialogue. In some parishes, people are already wondering how they will manage without their woman curate when she has to move on ('a horrible prospect').

All of this, of course, raises an obvious counter point: the effect of women's priesthood on men in general, and on men priests in particular. Until 1994 the priesthood was the one area of work closed to women in this country: the one area in which skills right across the spectrum of what are normally considered male and female attributes could be employed only by men. The point has often been made that women should be priests because, for biological reasons, they have innate pastoring and nurturing skills. This is so obvious that a deeper point has apparently been overlooked. In cultural terms, might not the very power of priestliness have come from the paradox of a man doing what is in essence woman's work? None of us, whatever our physiological gender, is one hundred per cent masculine or feminine in our interests and aptitudes, but somewhere on a line between the two. In most societies we have been conditioned to develop those attributes considered best suited to our gender. But all around the world, in every faith system that is in any way based on sacramental, mystical or magical communication with an unseen god or gods, the male becomes the officiant by crossing over from maleness to the traditional female actions of offering food, caring for those in distress, and acting as mediator. He does not become female, but by adding female functions to his own masculinity becomes culturally hermaphrodite, or complete. And someone who is complete in him- or herself would seem to have power, like Tiresias of Greek legend. Perhaps all those silly references to 'men in frocks' are expressing a subliminal truth. But two things then result from the emergence of women as priests. When women are allowed to do this 'women's work' the power of that crossing over is simply not there. And the men for whom priesthood was the one way their female attributes could be valued as essentially male are suddenly ousted from that sanctuary.

Some of this is reflected in the observation by several people that the church, in allowing women into the priesthood, has somehow demoted men, has 'not properly valued the role of men in God's world'. Some say it has contributed to a current crisis of identity among men. 'Too many women are the breadwinners in the family; too many women are taking men's positions, to the detriment of men,' a middle-aged woman said. There was the accusation that the church, in ceasing to be the last bastion of male supremacy, was simply following an agenda set by 'the world' and specifically by feminists, and 'fully backed by non-Christians in the media'. There was the feeling that the church, above all, might have had the courage to resist, for the sake of men's sense of their own worth. One man wrote:

> Women have the wonderful but exclusive role of bearing and nurturing children. This alone gives them status in society; men no longer have such an essential role, for even the process of fertilising eggs has been reduced to a technological process and more and more women are eschewing marriage and permanent relationships. Thus it is important to preserve the functions of men as patriarchs, counsellors, leaders, guiders, providers and protectors ... if any self-esteem is to be preserved.

This sense of a fall in the value of men in society may be a factor in the pain that is being felt in some sections of the church now, though it is generally expressed as ecclesiological rather than social. Such sections are relatively small, but in some people the pain is quite intense. 'Mostly I don't speak about it,' one woman wrote; 'the Anglican Church has no need of encouragement for division, but since you ask, this last year has hurt even more than I thought it might ... Jesus' Apostles were men... For me it is no longer the Apostolic Church ... Now I belong nowhere.' However, she continues to go to her parish church. 'Some consider me unkind to our woman curate, people who do not understand that I do not love her any less. I'm sure that she has noticed no difference in our relationship.' She ends her sad letter, 'Pray for me and all those like me. There are more of us than you think.'

Another letter-writer, an evangelical, believes that the presence of women in the priesthood has simply increased clericalism and clergy dominance and 'inward-looking churchiness', at a time when the church should be working instead on 'proper involvement of the laity [including women] in shared leadership with the clergy', and recognising that 'leadership of the church in public life should come mainly from the laity'.

'He has destroyed our future,' an elderly woman said of the present Archbishop of Canterbury, whom she holds responsible for this change in the church. 'He declares a Decade of Evangelism, and then, before he can turn around, he has split the church in two with women's ordination. In no time at all he has called me a heretic because I don't accept it. I am not a heretic.' A woman of obvious vigour and strength of character, she feels 'desperate, devastated'. She lives in fear, she says, of a woman priest giving her the sacrament when she is dying. Her parish church had voted not to have a woman vicar or a woman celebrant, and she stated that she would not wish to go to a church where a woman had ever celebrated. She was upset that a member of her family, who had recently moved, now found himself having to travel twenty miles to a 'safe' church every Sunday.

A woman who admitted that her reactions to the ordination of women were more from the heart than the head wrote: 'If one were in a parish where a woman vicar was appointed and one had no transport it would be a very painful situation.' The fact that her husband had been a theologian and, as she says, could himself see no theological objections to it, seems not to have lessened her distress. A man from a group of rural parishes wrote: 'The sense of isolation and lack of confidence experienced by many who remain unable to accept the church's action ... is a daily reality that only God can heal.'

In an anglo-catholic parish that has voted never to have a female incumbent nor female celebrants, the situation was described by parishioners as 'bad', and painful. Although they pride themselves on being never less than welcoming to women clergy – and I can vouch for that – they have noticed that fewer such women now come to their well-known centre of pilgrimage. They attribute this to the women's own perception of the situation rather than to any lack of warmth on their part. But it is hard to see how it could be otherwise.

Several from the catholic or evangelical wings of the church spoke of being marginalised. Many spoke of loss of unity, either within families (two opposing views on this subject was seen as more painful than differing political views) or within parishes or among friends ('One feels less able to speak freely to fellow Christians for fear of hurting or offending them'). A man who described himself as 'a person who cannot easily change course' said that he found himself having to go where 'the old tradition has not yet been outlawed'; but that he misses his friends at his parish church who are 'too kind, and profess to miss me'. He envies them, he says, 'for being able to accommodate every change'. But one woman actually found that her change of church, occasioned by her parish church's 'very hurtful' attitude to women priests rather than by a basic disagreement on the matter, has changed her and her husband's lives completely – and for the better. Her husband, who had not been a church-goer 'because of the influence of the Vicar' is now with her on the PCC of their new church.

Loss of unity in the eucharist was mentioned by some. An evangelical wrote: 'I can no longer approach the eucharist with a sense that it is a common unitative service. I want to attend my parish church, but I have decided not to receive communion when a woman priest is the celebrant or gives out the bread and wine.' This last phrase suggests that there is more here than merely an objection to women's priesthood, since authorised women have for a long time been able to administer the sacrament.

It is difficult to avoid seeing plain misogyny in some comments. Those women who have now become priests are sometimes seen in caricature mode, as having schemed and manipulated the church to get where they are. 'They'll want to be bishops next,' an evangelical man said. 'I can't imagine a woman bishop. I prefer a man. But I do accept that there will be ambitious women who will eventually say, "I want to be a bishop".' Anti-women feeling is not of course limited to male speakers. 'I felt a little bit sad,' said a woman from the same parish, 'when the vote went through [in 1992], that women were yet again in the forefront, that women were going to muck up the church.'

Priesthood means different things to different people. How it is perceived became evident in these interviews without being discussed directly. Most people's opinions about what is happening to the church showed a fairly functional view of priesthood, in which women either can or cannot, for scriptural or pastoral or practical reasons, do the work of a priest. Only anglo-catholic lay people suggested a different understanding: for them priesthood was more essentially about being than about doing, and a priest someone set apart and 'other'.

As the Church of England faces up to its financial problems and to social change, an awareness of the need for new forms of ministry does seem to be spreading out from bishops and diocesan offices to the parishes. Not surprisingly, the places where the idea of collaborative ministry has been most readily accepted tend to be also the places where the ministry of women has been accepted. But where the authority of one male leader is treasured and nurtured, and clearly filling a need of the parishioners, there is opposition to women as priests or leaders. This need for a single male leader shows up at either end of the church's spectrum: it can be as strongly present in a high anglo-catholic parish as in an extremely evangelical one.

'The Bible tells us clearly that the male has authority,' a man in an evangelical parish said. 'It's there in Timothy 2: a woman should learn in silence and humility, and should not teach. Adam was created before Eve.' This bible-quoting conflicted with a view expressed a minute or two earlier, that women could be very valuable in the church, preaching and teaching, even being deacons, but they should not be vicars, should not have authority. A young woman suggested that a woman in a pulpit has authority. The differences between leadership, authority, and being a vicar were not clear. An older man seemed to think it safer to bar women from all such dangers. 'I know women can be equally clever. But there are roles for men, and roles for women. We're happier with a man, here.'

Though it does not use the word 'headship', the ultra catholic wing of the church also finds the subject of male leadership a powerful one. 'For me, the priest is very much the Father of his people, and the father is the head of a family – though not in any sense of dominance or superiority,' says one correspondent. Another wrote: 'There is a basic difference between men and women – we were not created to do the same work. This is confirmed in many areas of both Testaments.' Another: 'Women are not natural leaders – exceptions are Boadicea and Mrs Thatcher.' (Mrs Thatcher was often mentioned by opponents of women priests, regardless of what one sensed to be their political affiliations.) And: 'The effect of our new curate is most noticeable for we have girlish giggles, yes, but no firm direction.'

The question of the pull between head and heart is particularly relevant here. At both ends of the church an institutional preference for male authority is being backed up by intellectual arguments that are often second-hand and in some cases barely understood. 'Do we listen to the Bible, or our feelings?' a man in his thirties asked. 'In this church we have a lot of [non-ordained] women's ministry. But in your head, you know that the Bible clearly tells that Man has authority. Even though I might feel that having a woman leader would be wonderful, the Bible tells me that Man has the headship.' A woman responded: 'That's true of many of us. We want to believe that women can be leaders. But we are evangelical.' As well as rejecting women's ministry, such parishes will reject real collaborative ministry. Token gestures may be made but what the people want, and probably what the priest wants to provide, is a strong father-figure to lead and direct them.

But in a middle-of-the-road group, with quite some years of experience of women's ministry, one man said that he was hopeful that women priests would alter the way priesthood was viewed, moving it away from concepts of authority. 'Vestments, for example,' he said, 'have come from governors in the Roman Empire. Priesthood belongs to the whole people of God.' He felt that pre-Christian ideas of an authoritarian priesthood had been reintroduced: 'Jesus turned things upside down, and we busily put them back up again.'

Even within the groups most opposed to women being in positions of leadership there are people who are asking questions. In an evangelical setting, an older woman found relevance in the fact that she had worried when she was asked to chair the local school governors, because all but one of the other governors were men; in time she realised her gender simply did not matter. In the same group a younger woman, who said her woman boss at work was 'the most organised, caring, switched-on person in the organization', asked why, if women can be in positions of leadership in the secular world, it is not all right in the church. She did not seem very convinced when another woman said that a vicar with parishioners is responsible for 'the whole of life', whereas a headteacher, for example, is only responsible for the children in her care. The young woman returned to her concern. If we are all equal in God's sight, she asked, why was there this one taboo area? If someone is called by God then it did not matter whether they were male or female. One or two of the other women present picked this up. 'God gifts people!' one of them said. 'If he had not meant women to have this role would he not have indicated that by not giving women the gifts of leadership?'

This question of women's gifts exercised many, in letters as well as interviews. Those opposed to the existence of women priests were typified by one who bewailed the 'loss' of a particular woman to the priesthood. 'If she had stayed as a deaconess, think how much she could have done! We could really use her.' The woman in question was still resident in the parish; but her gifts apparently cannot now be used. A correspondent wrote about the tension between normal courtesy to a woman and having to refuse to endorse something about her that is extremely important to her: her priesthood. 'This is particularly heightened when I can see the individual has gifts that could well be made use of by the church – but not as a priest.'

That sexuality plays a part in people's attitude to priesthood was only occasionally mentioned. One person made a link between repressed homosexuality and opposition to women priests. One man began his letter with the previously mentioned passage from chapter 2 of the first epistle to Timothy: 'A woman should learn in quietness and full submission. I do not permit a woman to teach or have authority over a man; she must be silent.' He did not, he said, necessarily subscribe to this in the secular world; but the church was a different matter. He continued:

> Women do not understand how men perceive the nature of relationships between men and women. They are rarely neutral and almost always overlain with sexual implications. This will get in the way of any pastoral role a woman may take with men in the church. A man is much more likely . . . to be neutral in the eyes of his flock.

This seems a strange assumption, after the centuries of female adulation of priests and curates that literature portrays and that most church-going women, if asked, find it difficult to deny. In one woman's verbal account of her distress at the thought of women priests the physical aspects of the gender of the priest seem very strong:

> I feel that a man, a man's voice, is very important to me. I feel there are enough women in church, they don't have to be priests as well . . . I wasn't against A. herself, it was because she was a woman, not a man . . . In the past I never ever thought, 'Who's taking the service?' If the Vicar's not a 'draw' it doesn't matter: I go because I want to worship in church . . .' [Once, in another country] the hostess at a meal was a woman priest. She asked me 'Why don't you like women priests?' There's nothing theological about it. I just don't like the voice. Christ was a man . . . To have a man celebrating is Christ. To me, a woman – rings, earrings and things – is not Christ.

But later, in the same group, a sensitively indirect response to this came from another woman: 'Is it a representation of Christ who gives you the bread [in the communion service], or is it the servant of Christ who is giving you *Christ*?'

It is often said that this first generation of women in the priesthood have had no role models. They have had to find out for themselves how to take on this hitherto male role without losing either the essence of what priesthood is, or their own individual qualities. Laypeople are clearly aware of this.

Writing of the ministry of several women in her parish, a woman wrote: 'It has heightened our perception of the priesthood, so that the male priests in the parish have to be able to empathise in ways which perhaps have been foreign to them. In this area women have brought a distinctive quality to the priesthood, and brought feeling more into the public arena.'

The caricature of a forceful and aggressive woman minister seems to be fading. Possibly the sting was drawn by *The Vicar of Dibley*, television's series about a lovely but terrible woman vicar who must have been an amalgam of everyone's worst fears. Nevertheless, many in the groups agreed that some of the American women priests seen on television years ago were not good for the cause. Robert Warren, the Church of England's National Officer for Evangelism, has said that 'Women entering a "man's world" often initially develop male ways of doing the job. How else will they be accepted? Only in the second and subsequent generations is there an expression of the authentically feminine contribution to the role' (*Church Times*, 23 September 1994).

There was a fairly general view among those who accepted the existence of women priests that they should be feminine priests and not ape the male. 'I liked what our Bishop said when he told women to bring their femininity to the job. I agree that we don't want second-class men,' wrote one woman. But the areas in which this femininity is to be expressed is a contentious matter. In particular, the question of clothes causes much distress or indignation. When I was first ordained deacon a letter of mine in the *Church Times* about the need for more womanly clerical shirts produced, as well as many helpful letters, the following anonymous contribution: 'Obviously you and your ilk want lace, frills and sequins, preferably designed by the equivalent of Dior. P.S., Don't forget the earrings and bracelets. – Have you never heard the word "humility"?' It was the matter of earrings that provoked the ire of a more recent male correspondent, talking about women priests generally: 'Wearing earrings at the Lord's table!' he wrote indignantly. 'Plus of course lipstick. When I think they should be holy.' Another writer was more moderate but made a similar point. 'When one sees women priests on TV with coloured blouses or long earrings it denigrates this office, to my mind. Women police and forces and nurses wear their uniform with pride ... leaving personal adornments for off-duty hours.'

I raised this topic at one of the group discussions, in a parish with some limited experience of women's ministry. They came to a conclusion that a clerical collar was not a uniform, but a statement, where necessary, for identification ('A collar means you are approachable'). They also made the point that a priest was never 'off duty', even when she or he was having a day away from work.

One correspondent was concerned about women's voices, urging serious voice production sessions for every woman priest. 'You ladies must get your act together. It is essential you overcome the natural weakness of voice.'

Fears continue that women's participation in priesthood will lead to changes in theology and liturgy.

> Our liturgy is now at risk. Once the feminist sentiments, that have been imported with women priests, take a hold then male references will be expunged (not female ones of course). If Christ was the Son of God then He was all-knowing for all time, past present and future, and would have appreciated the rights of women in all circumstances and yet He persistently spoke of the Father. Still, the women's movement knows best and I expect that soon I will be required to say 'Our Mother, which art in heaven . . .'

However, in practice no one had any instances of this to quote. From a parish with two women priests a laywoman wrote:

> Neither the quality nor the nature of the eucharist has been diminished with the advent of women priests . . . because neither woman has felt it necessary to alter the service . . . In time they may want to change things, but hopefully this will be because they feel that change is needed to improve the worship, rather than because of their sexuality, or as an ego trip or whatever.

This is not to say that women are not contributing, with their male colleagues, to ongoing changes in liturgical practice, or in theological thinking. Without doubt they are. But people in the parishes where it is happening are not complaining, which suggests that it is being done with sensitivity, with consultation and co-operation.

If the women are changing priesthood, priesthood is itself having an effect upon the women. Many speakers and writers mentioned the way the women had seemed to grow after their ordination. A woman who knew two new women priests wrote:

> The effect of priesting on one of the women has been most marked. Once she had internalised, and made her own, the fact of her priesthood, she began to flower. It's difficult to express what has happened, but she has grown so much, and yes, flowered, that it is a joy to behold.

One man spoke of a priest he knew who had said that she identified herself with her priesthood. 'That's good,' he said. 'With some priests, there's themselves and there's the priesthood. They're not integrated.' But some laypeople feel that women have to work harder to be considered good enough for the job. 'They are more obvious targets if their ministry is perceived in any way defective (inefficient, slow, etc.) . . . They are constantly under the microscope.'

Others think that the new priests are having a hard time, particularly when parishes which have not formally barred themselves from women's ministry nevertheless do not accept a woman incumbent when one is offered. A member of the 'Forward in Faith' movement, which is opposed to the priesthood of women, said he had heard two very senior members of the movement saying that 'the women are being let down by the laity' on this matter. Among the moderate groups interviewed there was considerable irritation at the fact that one no-saying parish often now prevents the possibility of a female incumbent for a whole group of parishes. They also suspected that a disproportionate number of women, compared to men, were working in effect full time for the church without any financial support from it. On the other hand the sometimes precipitate promotion of, and awarding of titles to, certain women priests – although at first greeted with delight by their supporters – was beginning to be seen as attracting considerable hostility from some male clergy. It was encouraging that the people who commented on this seemed to think the women could cope with these reactions.

Anxieties for the women, that were expressed in those weeks immediately after the first priestings, have lessened. One or two people remembered worrying, when someone walked out of a church on discovering that a woman was to celebrate Holy Communion, that the woman herself would be upset ('I hoped she hadn't noticed'). Now the women are stronger. It was from several shocked laypeople that I heard of a recent incident where a woman priest, processing at the induction of a new incumbent in a very anglo-catholic parish in her deanery, was audibly hissed. The woman herself was not bothered by it.

'The Team Council has given me a list of celebrants. So now we have to consult this, to see which church we can go to.' This is how one woman and her husband, in a group of rural parishes, deal with a situation they do not like. Most of the people from those parishes who had gathered to talk to me felt that the provision of such a rota was a fair way of caring for those troubled by the presence of women among the local clergy. In a place without such a list one man, who presumably would have gone to his own parish church whenever the celebrant was male, now has to go for safety's sake to another village.

'The church can make this work,' said the Lay Chairman of a deanery synod. 'And I am quite prepared to make sure it does work.' Planning is all-important, he said, and it is the responsibility of the parishes to produce lists of celebrants and preachers, and to make it quite clear where they stand. Although he cannot in conscience accept the priesthood of women he has found his Rural

Dean, who does accept it, to be very understanding: so that he is not expected to be present when a woman is being inducted to a parish. He is a member of 'Forward in Faith', and adds: 'It has said we must make sure that we don't fall out with people.'

A sad tale was told by one letter-writer, an evangelical with many anglo-catholic friends who finds himself in what he describes as 'a middle of the road church with a Rector tending to Sea of Faith radicalism'.

> Most members of the congregation have no sympathy or appreciation of why someone like me takes the view that I do. This general lack of understanding is fairly widespread in the deanery and the diocese, although the Diocesan Bishop and one of his suffragans have been very understanding and committed to finding a space for us, but it can't hide the basic fact that we are on the margins . . . At diocesan level, it is difficult to retain one's integrity and still operate effectively. For example . . . at Bishop's Council where the issue of women priests is relevant it is well understood that we have to largely proceed as if the subject is not relevant. It is not good manners to raise it.

He has found the existence of the groups 'Reform' and 'Forward in Faith' helpful; although his view of the latter is that it encourages members to withdraw from any contact with ministers who work with women priests.

There were mixed feelings among those interviewed about the efficacy of the system by which parishes are able to state, after a vote, that they do not wish to have a woman incumbent, and/or that they do not wish to allow a woman to celebrate in their parish. In one parish I visited there had been no prior doubt as to the virtual unanimity of the outcome: the vote had been taken and both resolutions passed. But they spoke aprovingly of a neighbouring parish, where it had been decided that it would 'be proper not to vote, because that would further divide the parish'. Another nearby parish was still trying to decide whether to vote. 'I think', one of the people said, 'that a number of priests hesitate to put the resolutions to the PCC because they might be passed by a small majority, and that would be divisive.'

One woman told me of a friend who had been very badly affected by her parish church voting through both these resolutions. 'The PCC vote tore her apart. She was very active in the church. But after the vote she began to back off, saying that women had no place in the church.' She seemed to lose heart and died shortly afterwards.

Several of the groups I talked with had heard of instances where the resolutions passed by one small parish within a benefice had then precluded the possibility of a woman incumbent for the whole benefice. Regardless of their views on women priests, none of them thought that was good.

In fact, support for the feelings of women clergy sometimes came from unexpected quarters. In a very anglo-catholic parish a former teacher and vicar's wife said,

> I feel very sorry for many women priests. I think the ground was not sufficiently prepared within the church as a whole. Many women seem to be going into jobs sideways, through chaplaincies and so on. Specialist ministries are very valuable, yes, but when women go into specialist ministry it looks as if they can't go into parish ministry. I blame the parishes, who don't choose women when they could.

The same woman mentioned a churchwarden from another church who was desperately telephoning around to find a celebrant for Christmas Day. When it was suggested that he contact a particular woman priest his reaction was a definite 'No'. He had nothing against it himself, 'but in this church I wouldn't take the risk'.

Opinions on how the church is coping with the changed situation varies not just from parish to parish but also within groups who share a common stance. 'I think this parish is dealing with it quite positively,' said a man in a parish which had passed both resolutions. But a moment later his neighbour said 'We have been five years in a state of siege. There has been no outgoingness.' And another woman in the same group said that when she went to a hairdresser in a nearby town, and was asked where she came from, the hairdresser said, 'There's been a lot of trouble there, hasn't there? I won't go to church any more.'

It is in places where the ministry of deaconesses and women deacons has been experienced for years that the least upset has been caused. 'The attitude in the parish has long been, "Why not? For heaven's sake get on with it",' a reader wrote.

> There was great rejoicing when the [1992] vote was carried, and we looked forward to the day when it would happen in this diocese. Life has not always been this straightforward. A few have found the ministry of women difficult to accept. They have either tried it, and stayed with us as a result, or gone to another parish. We have tried to be pastorally sensitive to their needs, but in the end the decision is theirs.

Someone whose parish was part of a team ministry said, 'We haven't been troubled about it at all. We're used to a team, so we haven't had a figurehead; it doesn't matter who [the officiant] is.'

'I was dead against women priests twenty years ago': so many comments like that invariably continue '. . . but then . . .' The conversion stories have generally had one thing in common: the experience of the ministry of one or more women. This is so widely recognised that many of the people I talked with were impatient for the church to take advantage of it. 'Parish priests should arrange swaps,' said a man in a parish with no women priests, 'so that their people can experience the ministry of a woman priest. That's how people change their minds.'

People talked about the changes in themselves. 'I was very unsure about it at first', from one woman, brought a chorus of 'A lot of us were', 'It does take some getting used to', 'But now it doesn't matter if it's a man or a woman!' One woman there said: 'When the vote was passed I thought, this is it, I leave my church. Then I got to know X., she changed me round completely. We're very lucky to have her.'

A woman who had always felt that the ministry of women was non-scriptural went 'in fear and trembling' to the first celebration by the new woman priest in their parish.

> During the service, it came to me very plainly, that this has got to happen. I went in feeling 'No way', I came out feeling it was right and proper. It was nothing she said. – It's very hard to go against what we were brought up with. It's only when you have a sudden spiritual insight, if you like, that this goes away.

A man who, from disapproval had come to approve wholeheartedly of women priests, wrote:

> I hope and pray that those who are bigoted and intolerant may come to realise that christianity is about LOVE! Dare I say this? – my late father once admitted to me that he had met clergy within the

Church of England that he felt had no 'calling' whatsoever. I cannot imagine any woman offering herself for ordination who did not feel she had a genuine vocation.

There was some speculation in the groups about people who are unwilling to change. 'Those who are against will avoid encounters [with women priests] – a pity!' 'Many people are prejudiced against when they have too little contact with women priests – a vicious circle.' 'Is it just laziness? It's easier not to change. People like things always how they were.' 'If people are against it, they think it's all to do with feminism.' One woman made a comparison with the problems of an earlier generation:

> My grandmother believed that she would be physically sick if she ate with someone from Africa: she believed that for seventy or eighty years. Then she met friends whose family had intermarried, and everything changed. She was so upset that she hadn't seen the light before.

One person, out of all these calls, letters and interviews, mentioned prayer. Her response was moving. Basically she is not in favour of women priests. But: 'It is very, very hard,' she said. 'I want to do what the Lord wants. It is painful. Our Rector said to me, "Do pray about it".' She can feel her thinking changing, and my enquiry makes her think further. 'Maybe this is the way the Lord is showing it to me.'

'The church is an animal that has worn out a lot of hammers!' The woman who said that was part of a group with quite differing views, and it helped to have her put their disagreement into a historical perspective. Straight away someone else said that in fifty years time people would think there had been a lot of unnecessary fuss over this issue. In another parish an elderly man said, 'Now we've got ordained women people will accept it more. It's us older ones that have the problem. In the future, the numbers against will diminish.'

The number who spoke of concern for the health of the whole church was encouraging. One of them was from a 'Forward in Faith' parish: 'We did not anticipate some of the consequences . . . The most serious aspect of all this is the damage to the church.' From the other side came a similar concern: the woman who had been distressed about someone walking out of a woman priest's service said, 'It really hurts, that someone could do that to the church.' Another woman, in another group, said of a similar situation: 'The sacrament is part of our faith. Not to go to Holy Communion just because it was a woman [celebrant] would be dreadful!' These are surely significant statements: and were perhaps summed up by the man who asked, 'Is [the current situation] something to do with the fact that we continue to believe in God, that the love is still there, life goes on? Christ is the foundation of our faith, is alive today despite controversy, is still our light.'

Most people with an overview of the dioceses of the Church of England – and of course these are mainly clergy – will say now that for the great majority in the church the presence of women priests has become an accepted reality. The issue has in the main ceased to be contentious.

But areas of need remain: areas of pain, of indignation, of uncertainty. From these interviews with a wide range of church-goers, and from the letters and calls of others, I would draw the following conclusions. Firstly, that the provisions that have been made for those who cannot for whatever reason accept women's priesthood are on the whole as just and as workable as they can be, with the inevitable consequent inequities fairly shared by both sides; although actual pain is now borne more by those in the minority position. Secondly, that the existence of a head–heart split in many people on this issue has to be faced if they are not to become spiritually ill over it; and since the input from the head is largely synonymous with the teaching they are receiving from their clergy, this responsibility is surely the clergy's. And thirdly, that when everything is taken into account, the outlook is bright; of all the views I have heard on this issue, that which gives the most hope for the future is the determination, frequently recurring in different forms, that the Christian faith and the Christian church overall is more important than this – under eternity – relatively minor division.

## 2  What difference is women's priesthood making to women?
PAMELA FAWCETT

*There was once a university lecturer who would not admit to the presence of women in his classes. He always opened his discourse with the words, 'Good morning, Gentlemen', in spite of the presence of a substantial number of women in the seats in front of him. This was set in the late thirties, at the outbreak of the Second World War. Soon many students were conscripted to serve in the forces and, as a result, the ratio of women to men in the college classes greatly increased. One day there was only one solitary male present among the strong contingent of women and the lecturer began, 'Good morning, Sir'. Eventually, this lone male was called up to serve his country in the armed forces and the assembled women waited to see how they would be addressed. 'Because there is no one here today,' the lecturer said, 'there will be no class,' and he walked out.*

I have discovered that this is how many women have perceived their place in the church. Of course, like most parables, it expresses a truth in very clear-cut terms and over-simplifies to make a point but the long-standing invisibility of women is now being acknowledged. They have been in the majority in most congregations for years but their role has been to listen, to pray and to fill the collection plate. Older women have no difficulty in remembering the time when lesson readers, choir

© 1996 Pamela Fawcett

members, servers, churchwardens were all male and sidesmen were indeed men (and not 'persons'!). That the clergy were male went unquestioned and the fact that masculine language was used in the liturgy to refer to the human race was part of the culture of the Anglican Church into which they were admitted by baptism and confirmation. It is a good job that the clergy did not act out the extreme position of the university lecturer, because, if they had done so, there would have been cancelled services followed by a general collapse of the church as its chief props were removed.

I have come across many women who can remember this scenario and who also remember, with surprise at themselves, that they did indeed accept it. But many would now admit that they were not nourished by it and may even have been damaged by an institution that was not able even to name them as being present in the most sacred moments of liturgy and worship. I have heard moving testimonies to this from women of a wide range of age and background. I shall re-tell some of their stories and offer some reflections on them.

I shall start with Jenny (not her real name), who is now in her sixties, because I found her story very powerful. She has been a practising Anglican since her confirmation and is highly intelligent with a long-standing interest in theology and devotional reading. She was able to rejoice in her marriage and the birth of her first child as being God's will for her life; the traditional woman's role of wife and mother seemed good to her. The words of the Magnificat were, she told me, a natural expression of her joy and fulfilment in a happy marriage and young motherhood. Her own much loved mother died after a distressing illness and she was able to care for her, supported by her husband, the clergy and the local congregation. Her faith made sense of this grief-laden experience, although it did not remove the sorrow as she commended her mother into the keeping of their heavenly Father. In all these life experiences she felt, and indeed was, supported by the church and the faith she had learned through it.

And then something different happened. Jenny lost her next longed-for baby through an unexplained late miscarriage. She naturally turned to the clergy, the Gospels and her received faith for sustenance but she found none. Her husband gave her good support but was bewildered by her sadness and, even more, by her turning away from the church that had always meant so much to her. She had been taught that Jesus, because he was truly human in every respect, experienced all human pain both mental and physical during his earthly life and therefore is able to present the griefs of the world to our heavenly Father in his own person. But how could he understand how a woman feels at a time like this? All the teaching Jenny had received, from childhood onwards, had emphasised the masculinity of Jesus: his strength, his power to command even evil spirits, his leadership, his youthful manliness. Feeling that her body had let her down at its most womanly centre, she also felt deeply that her religion had let her down – or perhaps that it had never really held much for the part of her that was essentially female or for the female part of the human race. She continued in the habitual practice of church-going and was certainly sustained by it although, she says, it did not feel like it at the time. Her gradual return to a living faith was enabled by her reading the women mystics, particularly Teresa of Avila with her honesty, humour and strength and Julian of Norwich with her vision of Jesus as a loving, sustaining mother. When the debate about women and the priesthood first reached her ears her lifelong experience as a member of a patriarchal church made her feel that this could never be, but there was a corner of her heart that longed for the inclusion of women in the priesthood and for the church to thereby validate women's truly human experiences. I was deeply moved to hear how, now that the priesthood in the Church of England does, at last, include women as well as men, she has been able gradually to accept the ministry of a woman priest and to re-live, in her mind, that painful experience of alienation from God and the church of her younger days. She has found that her pain at the loss of her baby and the death of her mother is accepted and absorbed within all the hurts of humanity by the love of a God who contains all that is good in motherhood as well as fatherhood.

The majority of the women I have spoken to have not recounted a specific incident which they see as a focus for their feeling of alienation, but they do speak of a feeling of 'rightness' and 'naturalness' as they see women at the altar or in pastoral situations. They speak of women's understanding of human emotions and an ease in expressing them that most men do not yet have. In this I hear echoes of Jenny's story. Furthermore, in so far as the priest, saying the words of consecration in the communion service, is saying them with Jesus Christ so is a new emphasis placed on Jesus' humanity when these words are spoken by a woman. Gone is the too narrow theology of the incarnation which saw Jesus' masculinity as normative. In its place is a rich, transforming understanding which is beginning to see the whole created order as mysteriously speaking the Word who was eternally made flesh at a moment in time nearly two thousand years ago.

Mabel is almost a generation older than Jenny. She is in her late seventies and slightly deaf. Otherwise, she is mobile, still driving her little Metro for local journeys which include church attendance on most Sundays and some week days. It does not come naturally to her to talk about herself but I soon discovered that she had not one but many stories to tell. She had some hair-raising adventures as an army nurse in the war, but did not want any of them repeated in a wider context than our informal conversation. I felt that her reticence in talking about this period of her life was due to a desire always to emphasise the good in human nature and not to perpetuate thoughts about the mess and horror of modern warfare. She had more to say about her children and grandchildren and about her experiences as wife and mother in a Christian family and community.

The most important person throughout Mabel's childhood was her mother. There was nothing amiss in her relationship with her father but he was fully occupied with building up and maintaining his business and seemed to be focused outside the family home. She was an only child, so her mother was her constant companion during the formative years that precede school. She remembers many little happenings with great pleasure: stories by the fire in the winter, learning to make pastry and bread, trips to the nearby city for shopping or exploration, cool churches and summer picnics in the park. This may sound too good to be true, but Mabel admitted to having been a naughty child. Perhaps it was the very gentleness of her mother that drove her to push the relationship to its limits. She recalls, with deep regret, that she sometimes reduced her mother to tears but, after such stormy episodes, the gentle, happy flow of life was always resumed without acrimony. One of Mabel's earliest memories is of her mother singing as she went about the routine household tasks. When she had been settled down for the night the sound of that pleasant, musical voice, rising from the kitchen, enfolded her in an atmosphere of love, peace and security that she still recalls with delight. When she herself married and had children her mother had died, but Mabel felt that the most important part of her lived on in the love with which she herself, although a very different personality, was able to surround her own children. And, what is more, she sees her own mother's loving nature reflected in her daughter's care for another generation of babies.

I asked her about her experience as an Anglican. She had little to say except to speculate that it must have been the opportunity to receive the sacrament of Holy Communion fairly regularly that kept her going through the war years and protected her from the dangers of army life – and she was not talking about sudden death or physical injury!

I observed that, although she had practised her religion diligently and helped willingly with church affairs, she showed a typically Anglican coolness and reticence when I tried to open up the subject of her personal faith. This is consonant with her reluctance to talk about her distinguished war career. She just did not care to talk about herself. However, she did return again to the singing of her mother that flowed through her childhood like the sap rising through the branches and leaves of a tree. 'The love of God is like that,' she said, 'if only we could always hear it.' After talking to Mabel, I was delighted to read confirmation of this experience in Wendy Robinson's booklet *Sounding Stones*,[1] where she writes about her mother's singing as being the context in which she learnt to be alone with God.

So although she had not articulated it, even to herself, until our conversation, Mabel now feels that all her varied experiences of motherhood – receiving, giving, observing – are part of her experience of God. On the occasions when she sees a woman at the altar she is reminded that

God is our Mother as well as our Father. She is still enjoying a new concept of the Godhead that is not only 'running the business' (like her own father) but is constantly, faithfully singing the mother's song of reconciliation and love for the refreshment and sustenance of all creation. Somehow, she says, the whole of her life makes better sense now that her church's priesthood is representative of the whole of humanity.

Not all the stories I heard had this joyful flavour. A few years before women priests became a fact, I was addressing a parish group on the subject of women's ministry. I knew that the majority of the people there were not likely to be sympathetic to women in roles of leadership, so my talk was very gentle and affirming of the tea ladies and the flower rota. At the end I invited questions. Silence! At last a hand went up at the back of the hall. My hopes rose; perhaps we were going to have a discussion after all. 'Don't forget that woman was created from only a very small bit of Adam,' said this not yet elderly lady. 'We must always stay in the background and support the men.' I think I spotted only one nodding head among the surprised audience, but no one had the courage to challenge her. Of course, I pointed to the other Genesis story, where men and women are equally created in the image of God. But I could see she was unimpressed. I have not seen her again but I have thought about her often, trying to understand the need which some women have to believe themselves inferior.

On the one hand, account must be taken of inadequate teaching in Sunday Schools by people who are not well informed about even the most basic biblical scholarship. From many pulpits, an almost fundamentalist faith is taught, for fear of upsetting the supposed 'simple' beliefs of some of the congregation. This means, for example, that the rich, layered meaning of the first two chapters of the book of Genesis is lost to people as a resource for understanding the human condition and its relationship with its Creator. And it means that people are not challenged to wrestle with the difficult aspects of Christianity and thereby to make their faith both real and personal.

In her book *The New Eve in Christ*,[2] Mary Hayter examines the creation stories in Genesis chapters 1 and 2. She concludes that the story of the creation of woman from Adam's rib is not intended to illustrate woman's inferiority and dependence but to emphasise the fundamental relatedness of man and woman – they are made from the very same stuff.

How the story continues of the woman I have described above, I do not know. But I have listened to the stories of women who started with a similar attitude. Although deeply convinced of their vocation to obscurity, they have been transformed and awakened by experiencing women in priestly ministry, and especially by their presidency at the eucharist. This is well illustrated by the story of Brenda. She is a widow with a strong biblical faith who does demanding work within a caring profession. She was filled with pain at what she saw as a departure from scripture when the first women were ordained as priests in her diocese. This pain was given an immediacy by the fact that the deacon in her parish, whom she liked and respected, was to be priested and would be celebrating the service of Holy Communion the following day. Against her conscience, and full of misgivings, she decided that she must be present at the service out of friendship and loyalty to her parish. Not to do so would have made her conspicuous in a benefice that was almost unanimous in its acceptance of the ordination of women. She could not find the courage to stay away, although it required an equal courage to attend. She felt that she would not be able to receive the bread and wine from a woman's hand, but she hoped no one would notice. She slid in on her own as the service was about to start. Gradually she became caught up in the familiar words and prayers and forgot that they were being spoken by a woman. When she looked up, it was a minister of the gospel that she saw at the altar; gender had ceased to matter. As a result of this and subsequent experiences, Brenda is beginning to see her own caring ministry in a new light, as part of that priestly ministry which belongs both to Christ and to the members of his body, the church.

Brenda's faith does not depend on a 'high' doctrine of the priesthood. Indeed, 'priest' is not a word that she uses to describe the clergy. That the twelve apostles were all male had convinced her that authority in the church was thereby reserved for men. She has now been encouraged to see the events of the earthly life of Jesus in their historical context. 'If Jesus came into our world now as a human being, I feel sure he would have chosen some women among the twelve,' she says. Brenda's faith has been renewed as a result of her new understanding. Jesus Christ is alive to her in a new and personal way.

Next is a story from the recent life of Rose. I do not know very much about her background except for the little she has been able to tell me from time to time over the few years that I have ministered to her in the nursing home where she now lives. The most important thing that I know about her is that the members of staff who are on duty always say, 'You can't start the service without Rose.' Everyone in the home knows that receiving the sacrament of Holy Communion is the most important event in her life. It always has been, even when she was a busy teacher and secretary of her Parochial Church Council. Now she is ninety years old and has completely lost her short-term memory, although she can still speak of a brother who was a priest and of Father B. and Father J. who had ministered to her in past times and in places which she cannot now remember. I first took Communion to the home as a deacon, using bread and wine that had been consecrated by a priest at an earlier service. I explained to Rose and, although it was strange for her to receive the sacrament from a woman, she was not troubled by it. She always said that it was a great privilege to receive the body and blood of Christ in this way, now that she could not attend church. I often had to explain again, as she never remembered that she had seen me before. The time came when I was able to conduct a full service of Holy Communion as an ordained priest. Rose was always there, in the same chair, and received her Communion with her usual gratitude. But one day she questioned me again. 'Have the bread and wine been blessed already?', she asked, as I prepared the table. I explained to her that I was now a priest, ordained by my bishop in his cathedral. 'Do we have women priests in our church now?', she asked. I assured her that we did, waiting nervously for her to decide whether to stay or seize her zimmer and leave the room. 'How really wonderful,' she said, 'I had no idea that women had come on so far. Now it is as though I am really in church again at a proper service.' She wondered what to call me and she thought it was funny that she could not call me 'Father' but did not seem to mind.

Although Brenda and Rose come from very different church backgrounds, Brenda an evangelical and Rose an anglo-catholic, they, in their own ways, have both transcended their respective traditions. The gender of the officiant was not important. What mattered to them was the presence of Christ in Word or Sacrament. It has been a great privilege to minister to Rose towards the end of her long life. Her faculties are greatly diminished but I never feel that she herself is diminished by her loss of memory and mobility. As she joins in the familiar prayers, she meets with God in the fullness of her identity, reflecting that image in which she was created.

This is the story of Maggy. She is the wife of the vicar of a busy suburban parish. She has two daughters and has spent the last ten years as a full time mother and part time, unpaid curate. She married her husband when he was in training for the church's ministry and greatly looked forward to supporting him in his valuable work. She has never complained about the way in which the parish so often intrudes on their family life, because she feels that her life and that of her daughters has been greatly enriched by the contact with such a variety of people, and she has always thought that it was her particular vocation to support her husband's ministry and to witness to Christian family values. Although parish life is never idyllic, revealing, as it does, so many human weaknesses, common sense and humour have seen her through and the shared experience has been a source of strength to a naturally strong marriage. Now that her children are both at school she has added some part-time teaching to her other commitments. While the girls were small Maggy was too busy trying to combine motherhood, home-making and some parish involvement to question the role of women in the Church of England. Her attitude of generous and happy indifference started to be eroded when she overheard the beginnings of the debate about the ordination of women when her husband discussed it with fellow clergy. She began to turn to the letters columns in the *Church Times* with an eagerness that she had not formerly felt for that journal. With all this came an invigorating sensation that her brain, long dormant beneath the demands of nappies, Barbie dolls, sleepless nights and exhausting days, was beginning to stir into life. And it was not just her brain that was coming to life; so was her awareness of the way in which the talents of half the human race were being pushed to one side by the church. The maleness of all the 'up-front' people in church government but, most of all, in the leading and organising of worship, suddenly felt like an affront to her and to all her sisters – those women who so faithfully kept the church show on the road from week to week by their presence and by their sacrificial giving. So she became a quiet supporter of the Movement for the Ordination of Women. If she had been alive at the time, she would have campaigned for the emancipation of slaves. In other words, for her, this was a justice issue. The arguments for and against women in the priesthood from tradition, biblical interpretation or theology were interesting but secondary to the fact that women's voices were not heard and their human experience was not valued. So what of Maggy now that women priests have been in place for over a year? There is no woman, as yet, on the staff of her parish, but that does not matter. Maggy is not a feminist; she does not want to see women taking over the church and marginalising the men. She is content to let the church evolve to a greater equality of status and opportunity and, meanwhile, she feels that the air is cleaner and the church as a whole has an openness about it which was not there before. She herself feels refreshed and invigorated by this new atmosphere. 'At last it is OK to be the mother of daughters,' she said with a smile as I parted from her.

I have tried to speak to a few women who are not church-goers or believing Christians. I had heard that some who fell into this category have been affronted by the thought that the role of 'vicar' could now be taken by a woman. However, I did not encounter any such views. Among the older women to whom I spoke I found nothing but a resounding indifference to everything to do with the church. It was not part of their lives or culture and they had better things to think about. Women under forty, perhaps because they had experience of the work place, were more interested in the idea of an 'equal opportunities' church. 'About time too' was a not infrequent comment. One even remarked that the Church of England had regained some credibility at last and perhaps it might now be listened to a bit more positively. I hope she is right. The idea of the church as being at last much more part of the 'real world' was echoed by one church-going professional woman in her thirties who said that, although she did not often encounter a woman priest in her church, she could not help feeling that there was a healthier and more 'normal' atmosphere at many church occasions.

The vision of a world in which women and men work, play and live in harmony, being enabled to use their great variety of God-given talents to the full and without prejudice, is still only a vision – and not even that in many parts of our society and the wider world. There are many places in the world where women are regarded as the personal property of their husbands. This may not lead to a life of hardship – most men instinctively care for their property – but it does imply a lack of freedom and choice that no self-respecting male human being would accept. Even in western society women's sexuality is exploited not just by brothel owners but by the advertising industry and, of course by all who collude with this. The Church of England and the church in many other parts of the Anglican Communion can now, at last, begin to embody that vision. It is a big responsibility and a great challenge to reflect to the world a picture of women and men together, created from the same dust and made equally in the image of the Creator God.

The issue of 'justice' which is brought out by Maggy's story (and others') is one that did not play a large part in the debate before the synod vote in 1992. There were more important aspects of concern: relationships with other denominations (and particularly with Rome), church and biblical tradition, the theology of creation, the doctrine of the priesthood. But outside of all this, for very many ordinary church-goers and even for some who were quite indifferent to religion, the injustice of barring women from the priesthood and therefore, as they saw it, from all authority in the church, loomed as large as the injustice of withholding the parliamentary vote from women until 1928.

The stories I have been using and the people in them are deliberately disguised, by changing the names and some of the details of their circumstances. It was only by assuring them that this would happen that they were able to talk freely and honestly. I am very grateful to all of them and hope that, if they read this, they will not only recognise themselves in what I have written, but also feel that others will not so recognise them.

After all this talk and much reflection on it over what now seems like a long space of time, I am beginning to see an emerging picture. It is of a variety of women, of all ages and from many different contexts, gradually learning to take hold of their own full humanity and adulthood. They have all started from different places but all seem to have been travelling the same road. I have met a few women who have not yet started the journey and can, usually, understand why this is so for certain individuals. However, these few do not detract from the momentous sight of women on the move, travelling at last alongside the men to make real the image of God in which they were created as individuals and as part of God's kingdom.

I started this chapter with a parable and I am going to end in the same way. During the space of time that I have been occupied with exploring my theme with as many women as possible, I have also been watching the beginnings of new life in my garden pond. So here is the parable of the frogs.

*The thin sunshine of early spring saw the comma-shaped tadpoles wriggle out of the comparative safety of the slippery frog-spawn and start searching for suitable food. Soon their bodies grew robust and their tails learnt a beautiful elegance of movement, an economical undulation that produced swift forward motion as well as sharp, evasive turns. The shaded water was their home. They explored its weedy corners and exposed edges as though they were going to live there for all their life-span. But they had to learn the lesson that the safety and cool greenness of the water was not their lasting home. As the summer sun warmed the water and increased the availability of food, the little swimming creatures began to grow legs and find within themselves an urge to haul out of the water on to the lily leaves. There was a strange, awkward period when their tails had begun to shrink and had lost their former swift elegance of movement, and their tiny legs were still too unformed to propel them forward by jumping across the leaves or by breast-stroking through the water. But at last, thanks to the life-force within each, the final stage was completed. Every lily-pad seemed to be the platform for a tiny, perfect frog, smaller than the hover-flies which visited the pond to drink. They could now claim the freedom of the earth. Many dangers will lie ahead and they still have several demanding years of growing and searching for food in order to reach their own destined maturity. Some, at least, will make it to produce the next generation. In such a way is the continuity of life assured. Although their way of swimming is now different, the little frogs will continue to enjoy the water of their home pond, especially in the extremes of weather. They will immerse themselves in its coolness in the heat of a dry summer and bury themselves in the mud at the bottom beneath the winter ice. But they will not be confined. For a time it will be hard for them to have to forget their beautiful, subtly rhythmical tails and the confines of their small pond but now they can leap and swim with four powerful limbs and take hold of the wide earth with delicate, strong hands.*

## Notes

1 Wendy Robinson, *Sounding Stones: Reflections on the Mystery of the Feminine* (SLG Press, 1987), pp. 5 and 6.
2 Mary Hayter, *The New Eve in Christ* (SPCK, 1987), pp. 99f.

# 3 What is priesthood?

RUTH WINTLE

> 'These are the garments they are to make: a breastpiece, an ephod, a robe, a woven tunic, a turban and a sash. They are to make these sacred garments for your brother Aaron and his sons, so that they may serve me as priests.' (Exodus 28.4, NIV)[1]

Thus God's instructions to Moses in the context of the setting up of the Tabernacle and its worship. The priestly garments of Aaron and his sons, symbolising the essence of priesthood, are a reminder of the 'sacredness' of those set apart by God to serve as his priests. Three times over, in the introduction to the detailed instructions for the priests' sacred garments, God says, 'so that they may serve me as priests' (Exodus 18.1–4). The service of God lies at the heart of all priesthood (cf. Numbers 18.7: 'I am giving you the service of the priesthood as a gift').

The ephod, with its onyx stone shoulder pieces, engraved with the names of the sons of Israel as a memorial, was the garment which came to symbolise the word and the wisdom of God imparted to the people through the priest. The breastpiece, 'for making decisions', was also engraved with the names of the twelve tribes of Israel, and contained the Urim and the Thummim, symbols of the priest's task of discerning God's will on behalf of the people. 'Whenever Aaron enters the Holy Place, he will

© 1996 Ruth Wintle

bear the names of the sons of Israel over his heart on the breastpiece of decision as a continuing memorial before the Lord' (Exodus 28.29; and cf. Ezra 2.63 and Nehemiah 7.65). As the priest presented the offerings of the people, in the tabernacle, and entered the inner sanctuary to burn incense and, once a year, to make atonement for their sins, so, wearing the ephod and the breastpiece, he carried the people into God's presence, to offer sacrifice and prayer, and to receive and to give God's blessing. 'So they will put my name on the Israelites, and I will bless them' (Numbers 6.22–7).

The robe, woven tunic, turban and sash all served as reminders of the God-given 'holiness' of the priest as he performed his priestly duties, protecting him from death in God's presence, and symbolising the purity which was his solely by virtue of God's calling and grace.

Set apart to serve, discerning God's will and safeguarding his word and his truth, standing before God to offer sacrifice on behalf of his people, counted as holy by God's choice and grace, blessed and blessing ... such was the priest of the Old Testament, albeit characterised by different emphases and tasks at different times in Israel's and Judah's history.

The Old Testament priesthood may seem a strange starting-place for an exploration of what priesthood is in the Church of England in the twentieth, nearly twenty-first, century. There is no overt continuity between the priesthood of first-century Judiasm and that of the Christian church. Jesus was not a priest; the apostles were not priests; the leaders of the early church were not priests. It was essential that they should *not* be priests, for one of the main Judaistic priestly activities was sacrifice and the early church knew no sacrifice other than that of Jesus on the cross. The early church leaders were appointed, in succession to the apostles, to teach, to lead, to give order and to hold together the faithful. Over the first few centuries of the church's life the threefold order of bishops, priests and deacons became the recognised order of leadership in the church. Within that order the 'priests' were originally 'presbyters', with an emphasis on 'eldership', but as the threefold order itself changed in a constantly growing and changing church, so the emphasis of the priestly ministry became more sacramental, more closely related to sacrifice, more central to the church's life. Bishops became more 'rarefied'; deacons became almost non-existent (though not in all churches), except as 'probationary' priests. In most western churches of the catholic tradition, a call to ordination is seen as a call to priesthood. While recognising that priesthood is 'being' rather than 'doing', the Church of England has tended to emphasise the functions of the priest in terms of his leadership (often confused with management) of the local church; his teaching, pastoral, adminstrative role; his 'separateness' from the laity, and his centrality to the life and worship of the church. However, at the heart of the 'hyper-activity' of the clergy, the eucharist continues as the pivot of priesthood, and embodies the unseen continuity between the priesthood of the Old Testament and that of Christendom.

The church, while rightly emphasising the uniqueness of Jesus, and of his priesthood, nevertheless encapsulates in the ordained priesthood something of the priesthood of Christ. The priest is seen as the 'icon' or as the representative of Christ, whether at the altar or as head of the church. Knowing that Christ has offered himself 'once for all' as a sacrifice for all sins, the priest, in the eucharist, offers the gifts of the people, a memorial of Christ's sacrifice, a sacrifice of thanksgiving and praise. Rightly guarding against the danger of seeming to offer again the life and death of Christ, the church has, also rightly, retained this sacrificial theme, which figures in its worship as the offering of praise and thanksgiving, as the offering of the worshippers' lives for sanctifying and for service. In this sense then, centred on sacrifice, there is an invisible link, a mystical link touching the very heart and essence of priesthood, between the priests of Christianity and of Judaism. Furthermore, going back to the roots of Old Testament priesthood, in the commands given to Aaron and his sons, we find the emphases, not only of offering sacrifice, but of being set apart to serve, of discerning and safeguarding God's Word, and of forgiveness, life and blessing received and shared, which continue as marks of priesthood in our church today.

Before ever these priestly attributes were spelled out for Aaron and his sons, however, the Torah had highlighted the special calling to priesthood of the whole people of Israel.

> Moses went up to God, and the Lord called to him . . . and said, 'This is what you are to say to the house of Jacob and what you are to tell the people of Israel . . . Although the whole earth is mine, you will be for me a kingdom of priests and a holy nation.' (Exodus 19.3–6)

The people were set apart to serve God; the people were to discern and to understand God's will and God's word; the people were to stand before God as his 'remembrancers' (a possible translation of Isaiah 62.6b) on behalf of the whole world; the people were called 'holy' by God's choice and grace; the people were to receive God's blessing and, in accordance with God's promise to Abraham, to be a blessing to all peoples on earth (Genesis 12.3).

While the Aaronic priesthood as such makes no appearance in the New Testament, the priesthood of the whole people of God is both implicit and explicit in many New Testament passages. Peter, notably, quotes directly from

Exodus when he reminds his readers, 'You are a chosen people, a royal priesthood, a holy nation, a people belonging to God, that you may declare the praise of him who called you out of darkness into his wonderful light' (1 Peter 1.9). It has become a commonplace, in the church today, to give emphasis to the 'priesthood of all believers', but we are only slowly, I believe, beginning to recognise that this is not just a new thought but a reality.

The concept of priesthood lies at the heart of Jesus' own ministry, not only in his unfolding of God's will and purpose and in his life of service to others, but in his very person, himself the Word, the sacrifice, the blessing. He does not use of himself the term 'priest', nor does he specifically call his followers to priesthood, but the life and language of sacrifice and of opening God's word to others is the life and language of a priestly ministry, and it is to this that Jesus calls his disciples. Sharing his cross and his cup, carrying his message and discerning his word, the people of the new covenant are surely conceived by Jesus to be a priestly people. This theme of sacrificial offering, and of presenting the whole of one's life as a liturgy, is taken up by some of the New Testament writers, notably by Paul in Romans 12.1 ('Therefore I urge you ... to offer your bodies as a living sacrifice, holy and pleasing to God – this is your spiritual act of worship'). The parallel themes of understanding God's word and unfolding his purpose to others, of living out God's forgiveness and blessing in his world, are implicit in New Testament teaching, and explicit in the letter to the Hebrews.

Even though Jesus neither called himself a priest nor called his followers to 'be priests', the priestly ministry which he exemplified and to which he did call his disciples is picked up and expounded by the writer of the letter to the Hebrews. The first 'priest' mentioned as such in the Old Testament is 'Melchizedek, king of Salem' (Jerusalem). He 'brought out bread and wine. He was priest of God Most High, and he blessed Abram' (Genesis 14.18). The writer to the Hebrews designates Jesus as 'high priest in the order of Melchizedek'. In a closely argued exposition, he describes the worship of the tabernacle and the role of the priest as symbols or templates of the reality of priesthood and sacrificial worship fulfilled in Jesus. Jesus does not stand in the Levitical line of priesthood. He supersedes it, stepping into that mysterious and mystical order of Melchizedek, 'without father or mother, without genealogy, without beginning of days or end of life, like the Son of God he remains a priest for ever' (Hebrews 7.3), the king-priest of Psalm 110. As high priest of this 'eternal' order of priesthood, Jesus opens the door for all believers to share in his priestly ministry of word and worship. 'Since we have confidence to enter the Most Holy Place ... let us draw near to God ... having our hearts sprinkled to cleanse us from a guilty conscience and having our bodies washed with pure water' (Hebrews 10.19–22). Through Jesus the great high priest we, too, are called to priesthood. 'Through Jesus, therefore, let us continually offer to God a sacrifice of praise – the fruit of lips that confess his name. And do not forget to do good and to share with others, for with such sacrifices God is pleased' (Hebrews 13.15–16). The New Testament is redolent with the priestly ministry of the people of God.

This renewed emphasis on the reality of the priesthood of all believers has created, in some parts of the church, two particular areas of concern. One is the way in which that 'priesthood' should be expressed in daily life and worship; the other is what it says about, and where it leaves, those whom the church designates as its 'priests' – its clergy.

I have been a Christian all my life (over sixty years), and have begun to glimpse and to understand something of what it means, as a Christian, to be a priest . . . sharing the priestly ministry of Christ. I have also been in full-time, 'ordained' (i.e. 'set apart') ministry for twenty-eight of those sixty-plus years, and, during that time have worked, as 'parish worker', deaconess, deacon and priest, in the fields of parochial, educational, administrative and diocesan ministry. For most of the twenty-eight years I have been involved with men and women preparing for the 'ordained' ministry. Inevitably I have been faced constantly and continuously with all the questions which arise in the selection and training of those whom God and the church 'call' to a recognised and 'set apart' ministry. The same questions have presented themselves over and over again. What does it mean to be 'priestly laity'? Why not serve God as laity? Why does the church have 'set apart' ministries? (I use the term 'set apart' rather than 'ordained', because the question applies as much to certain lay ministries, such as those of the Church Army officers, or Religious, as it does to deacons or priests.) What is distinctive about ordained priesthood?

In *A People of Priests* (DLT, 1995), Michael Richards sets himself the task of unravelling some of the confusions which have arisen in the Roman Catholic Church as a result of the emphasis given by Vatican II to the priestly role of the 'laity', particularly in respect of the relationship between 'ordained' priest and priestly laity. He sets out aspects of the problem and ways in which it has been approached, against the background of the crisis of confidence experienced by many of the clergy who feel that their distinctive role as priests has been diminished, or blurred. He says,

> This theme has so far been presented as if it were a

matter that only concerned the Catholic Church; a study arising out of our need to clarify our thinking about the ordained ministry in order to emerge from an identity crisis. But more is at stake than the simple survival or otherwise of a particular religious institution. On the solution of this problem depends the continuing presence and influence of Christianity itself. (p. 15)

In order to survive, the church must understand what it means to be priests, and what it means to have priests. Michael Richards continues,

> A priest is a worshipper. The words and gestures he uses are manifold, but their purpose is the same: to worship, to express and foster the relationship between his own life, together with that of the community to which he belongs and for whom he acts, to the values they hold in honour and the forces by which they are governed . . . All priests relate to what is holy: all holiness comes from the God who made himself known in Jesus Christ and in doing so called together a people of priests. (pp. 19–21)

I suspect that few Christians, of whatever denomination or cultural background, think of themselves as 'priests'; I suspect that few Christians think of themselves, primarily, as 'worshippers'. Centuries of development and change in Christendom have moved the emphasis of priestly life and activity to the 'ordained' minister. Centuries of changing emphases in Christian life and activity have given more prominence to moral rectitude, generosity to neighbours, witnessing to the truth, and church attendance, than to a reality of worship. In fact, of course, there is (or can be and should be) an element of worship in all of the above, but that is not, on the whole, where the emphasis is put, and most Christians, asked about the place of worship in their daily lives, would talk about 'going to church' or, possibly, about 'saying their prayers'. Few would say, 'I am a priest. As a priest I am a worshipper, and every aspect of my life is devoted to worship.'

As an 'ordained' priest, I also am, before anything else, a 'worshipper', and I see my central task as that of leading the priestly people of God, not only in worship, but back to an understanding of their own priesthood, as worshippers. 'Worship' (as priesthood) has many meanings and many different emphases. Without going into them in detail, I suggest that a 'worshipping' community of Christians might be recognised by its 'God-centredness'. As a gathered congregation it would concentrate on God's glory, remembering Peter's words, 'You are . . . a royal priesthood . . . that you may declare the praises of him who called you out of darkness into his wonderful light', rather than on its own fellowship or fulfilment. Too often, acts of 'worship' seem to become times of self-indulgence, of experience, or of education, centred on the participants rather than on God. Discovering what it means to 'worship' together as a congregation of 'royal priests', is almost certainly a never-ending process; but genuine awe, wonder, praise, thanksgiving, sacrificial offering, 'remembrancing' of the community and the world which we represent, discerning of God's wisdom and will, and a deep, silent wholeness of 'being' in God's presence, would surely come nearer to the truth of 'worship' than many of the activities which we put under that heading.

By extension, the congregation dispersed about its daily business, at home, at work, at play, continues in worship, doing all to God's glory and in his name – God-centred and not human-centred. It is easy to say, 'Those are just words, fine ideas, but what do they mean in practice? Life is too pressurised, too urgent, too competitive, etc., etc., to be thinking about God all the time!' But we also have a reminder that 'God is spirit, and his worshippers must worship in spirit and in truth' (John 4.24). It is significant that the last few years have seen a distinct move, at least in the British churches, towards spiritual development and depth, through spiritual direction, retreats and quiet days, study of devotional books, a desire to learn how to 'be' a Christian, rather than what to 'do' as a Christian, and a recognition that 'worship', in the place of work or leisure, springs out of a spiritual set of heart and mind. Integrity and worship are closely bound one to the other. The search goes on for what it means for the whole church to be 'a royal priesthood, a holy nation'.

The quickest answer to the second question, 'Why does the church have "set apart" ministries?', is that it always has done. The people of God in the Old Testament were called to be a people of priests, but they also recognised a 'set apart' priesthood, and various parallel strands of ministry such as Levites and prophets. The early church acknowledged the special position and authority of the apostles, and quickly appointed others to act as leaders, administrators and teachers in the churches. Alongside the apostles we find bishops and deacons; and the letter to the Ephesians refers to 'prophets, evangelists, pastors, and teachers' as though they were in some way recognised as 'orders' of ministry (Ephesians 4.11). Presbyters appear in the New Testament as 'elders', but only in the book of Acts and in the Pastoral Epistles, and not in parallel with bishops and deacons. They came quickly and increasingly into prominence, however, from the second century onwards, and the title 'priest' replaced 'presbyter' early in the church's history. Throughout the centuries the church has appointed and valued a variety of different 'set apart' ministries, both lay and ordained.

Such ministries were and are primarily functional –

Moses appointed 'elders' to share his task of 'judging' the people of Israel; Aaron was called by God to be a spokesman, and was then made 'priest' in order to perform the duties attached to the tabernacle. The Levites were given specific tasks, diaconal, musical and manual, to assist Aaron and his sons. The prophets were called to discern and proclaim the 'word of God'. (Some were paid, but it soon corrupted them because they were tempted to say what pleased their employers, rather than to adhere to the truth.) In the early church, deacons, bishops, evangelists, teachers, elders, all had specific tasks and were appointed to do a job. In many instances it was work which lay beyond the scope of most of the Christians, in terms of either ability or time. The letter to the Ephesians, quoted above, does give a strong hint, however, that the main thrust of the ministry of those 'set apart' was to enable the whole church to function, '. . . to prepare God's people for works of service, so that the body of Christ may be built up . . .' (Ephesians 4.12).

Throughout the church's life, those 'set apart' for distinct ministries have been those who have been called to concentrate on particular aspects of the Christian life such as prayer or evangelism, healing or prophecy; those who have been called to nurture, teach and enable the whole church, such as pastors and theologians; and those called to lead and to administer, such as bishops, priests and deacons – with vast areas of overlap in every direction, and a distinct tendency to concentrate everything (especially in this century) in the life and work of the (ordained) priest. Wherein, then, lies the distinctiveness of the ordained priest?

For many people, 'priest' equals 'vicar' (or 'rector'). The distinctiveness of the ordained priest lies in the fact that he keeps the church going. It is 'his' church. He is omni-competent and hyper-active, with a band of willing (or conscripted) church members to help him. For years (centuries?) church people (C. of E. variety) have been unable to envisage a church without a vicar, a church without a 'priest'. Too many tasks demanded of the 'priest' in order to keep the local church afloat have hidden the essentials of his priestly role. Thankfully, from time to time these essentials receive a renewed emphasis, and many priests work hard to keep them to the fore. The priest is there to teach the faith, to lead the worship, to administer the Sacraments, to care for the sick and needy, to reach out to the unbelievers, to represent the church in the community. These tasks are spelled out in the ordination service, summarised in the priestly designations of 'servant, and shepherd . . . messengers, watchmen and stewards'. Increasingly, however, as we recognise the significance of the priesthood of all believers, we discover that in any congregation or gathering of Christians there are gifted teachers and preachers, leaders of worship, carers and healers, communicators and evangelists, administrators, and those who are strong in prayer, and we wonder, again, about the distinctiveness of the ordained priest.

In the World Council of Churches 1982 report, *Baptism, Eucharist and Ministry*, the paragraph on the ordained priesthood summarises the task of the ordained in relation to the life of the whole church. Significantly, the term used in this report for the ordained priest is, in fact, 'presbyter'.

> Presbyters serve as pastoral ministers of Word and sacraments in a local eucharistic community. They are preachers and teachers of the faith, exercise pastoral care, and bear responsibility for the discipline of the congregation to the end that the world may believe and that the entire membership of the Church may be renewed, strengthened and equipped in min-

istry. Presbyters have particular responsibility for the preparation of members for Christian life and ministry. (p. 27 para. 30)

Priesthood is handing on the faith within the Christian community and witnessing to the faith in the wider community. There is a safeguarding of the faith in the ordained priesthood, a continuity of Christian truth and orthodoxy, an adherence to that historic strand of basic doctrine which holds the church on course. It has little to do with individuals, for ordained priests may be, or become, very shaky in their faith, and many who are not ordained retain and adhere to the truth more firmly than the clergy. Nevertheless, the handing down of the truth from one generation to the next remains as a continuous strand in the episcopacy and ordained priesthood of the church. It is, of course, vested in the episcopacy, but is distinctive, by extension, in the ordained priesthood and diaconate.

Priesthood is witnessing to the faith in the wider community. All Christians are called to witness, but there are times when that witness needs to be focused in a particular individual, or in identifiable representatives of the whole. The community needs to know who is the focal point of the church in its midst; to have, as it were, a point of reference, a contact, a visible sign of the Christian life being lived out within it.

Priesthood is a discerning of God's will, an understanding of God's word. The ordained priest, listening to God, leads her people in listening, imparts to them her insights, inspires them to draw closer to God and to share their insights with others. A listening clergy should both emerge from and create a listening church.

Priesthood is worshipping. A listening church becomes a worshipping church and a missionary church, for worship and mission must go hand in hand. A listening church will reach out to God in praise and in intercession; will reach out to the world to give it a sense of awe and to meet its deepest needs. The ordained priest, giving time to listening, to worship, to mission, focuses her people's priesthood, and, in that focusing, sets them free to be God's priests in his world.

Even as a deaconess and as a deacon, my own ministry was an enabling one, setting others free to exercise their own ministry, but it was largely a ministry of activity. It was a combination of doing certain things that most lay people did not do, particularly in the sphere of leading worship and preaching, and of giving a focus to many aspects of ministry which are shared by all Christians. In a church which has never given clear definition to a diaconal ministry, there was little outwardly to distinguish my ministry from that of my colleague who were priests, other than in the things which I could not do – consecrate, absolve and bless. As tutor in a theological college, ACCM selection secretary, and diocesan director of ordinands, I was working in contexts where most of my colleagues were priests, but where, in fact, for much of the time, there was little to distinguish our ministries one from another. In parochial ministry those distinctions would possibly have been more pronounced, but on the whole, because most clergy are priests, the activities in which I engaged – whether as deaconess or as deacon – seemed to most of those amongst whom I ministered to be 'priestly'. In terms of activity I was 'ordained' to serve the church, by teaching, praying, leading, encouraging, nurturing, whatever the actual context of that activity. It did not particularly matter whether I was ordained 'priest'; I was able to offer service and leadership in order to set the church free to make its own offering of worship and service in the world. The distinctiveness of my ministry lay not in priesthood but in ordination. I did not, in that diaconal ministry with its many 'priestly' emphases, recognise the lack of a 'priestly' dimension.

In 1993, when the ordained priesthood was open to women, I had no personal sense of calling, but I realised that in the eyes of many I was already a priest, and that I should in fact be denying my ministry if I failed to offer for priesthood. I became aware of the significance of that distinctively priestly dimension in my ministry in the first eucharist at which I presided. I prefer not to use the term 'celebrate', because the whole congregation joined in the celebration. I knew that I was saying the word of consecration on behalf of all who shared in that act of worship. If the words of the prayer of thanksgiving were not made alive so that all could be part of them, they would have no meaning. In saying the words of absolution, and in pronouncing the blessing, I found it hard to be, as it were, set over against the congregation. In both absolving and blessing I was conscious of the emptiness of my words if they were not both received and passed on by the congregation.

As the communion service is the hub of all worship, it is also the expression and the focus of the life of the church. It is the church listening to God; it is the church confessing its own sin and in its confession bearing the world's sin; it is the church opening the floodgates of forgiveness into the world; it is the church holding before God the world in all its need, the world in all its beauty and joy, ugliness and pain; it is the church entering into the mystery of incarnation and sacrifice, of resurrection and new life in the Spirit; it is the church equipped and revitalised to 'live and work' to God's 'praise and glory'; it is the church worshipping, working and waiting for the coming of the kingdom. As the wholeness of the church's life, of its priesthood, is focused in the communion service, so the president focuses that priesthood and holds it as an offering before God. I can only express my (ordained) priesthood as my serivce to the priesthood of the whole church. I stand for God's people before God, as they stand before God on behalf of the world. We are together priests, a 'holy people' set apart to praise God and to serve him. My calling is so to serve Christ's people that they may be set free in their service.

Priesthood is worship. Priesthood is sacrament. Priesthood is receiving the gift of life, offered in the body and blood of Christ. Priesthood is sharing that life with others. Priesthood is accepting forgiveness, and forgiving others. Priesthood is being blessed and being a blessing to others. Priesthood is all that the church is called to be. The ordained priesthood is a sacrament (an outward and visible sign) of the priesthood of the whole church (an inward and spiritual grace). The ordained priesthood is the setting apart of the few to be the focus of the priesthood of all. The ordained priesthood is called to set God's people free to be his priests, standing between God and his world; forgiven and forgiving; life-receiving and life-giving; blessed and blessing.

*Note*

1 All biblical quotations in this chapter are taken from the New International Version.

# 4 Recovering from gender stereotypes:

## Codeines and kite

An exploration of some of the social systems and stereotypes encountered by women priests living into communities of equality for women and men

MARY ROBINS

---

'My wife has come as house-mother, with a handbag full of codeines in case my talks are too heavy for you,' said the bishop during his introduction to the pre-ordination retreat of women to be priested. The women laughed. He was being his usual caring self and they were used to his ways of talking. His talks, in fact, fed and prepared them well for ordination. A house-mother was not much needed; nor were the codeines! Did the bishop need some way of saying that he had lived much of his life in a social system that regarded men's thinking and mental activities to be stronger than those of women, and therefore rather heavy for women? Was he, even unconsciously, aware that women may resort to an old habit of sexual control — that of a headache? Did he really feel he could not pastorally care for women who may need 'mothering'? Or was he exposing these stereotypes as he prepared to ordain women who would stand before God and the people they were to serve, in the fullness of their humanity: women, not defined as 'other' to men, but disciples of Christ

© 1996 Mary Robins

bringing all the embodied humanity with which they were created?

The kite drifted upwards, dived, recovered, flounced a little, while the women ordinands relaxed in the sun. Playful energy that longs to create, flow free, reach into God and return to the human body is imaged by the kite. Some women ask, a little fearfully, how space for this creativity they own will be claimed in the institutional church. Will it be considered dangerous as it was in the past?

### *New stereotypes for old?*

'I'm glad women have been ordained – it is good to have the weaker sex represented,' declared a generous incumbent, as he welcomed a woman priest to preach in his church.

'I expect you will be busy patching up the people the exchange vicar upsets,' says the archdeacon to a part-time woman priest. He is confused when she replies, 'No, he can do his own patching up!'

A woman priest said she would not be shouted down by her male colleague while she was leading worship. 'I like your passion,' he smirked. 'I will not have an act of worship violated,' she retorted.

'You are a school marm,' he mocked. 'Yes, isn't it useful to have that experience?' she quietly replied to her priestly colleague.

'She needed it, so I gave it to her,' explained a man priest who was struggling with the fact he had sex with a newly bereaved widow in his pastoral care. His woman priest colleague was furious with him.

'There is no domestic violence in my parish,' declared an incumbent. 'I know this because no one comes to me for help.'

The women in the above exchanges are coming into an awareness of themselves which no longer fits into the system in which the men are used to working. This awareness may be new in much of the church, but it is not new in other places. In her book *Women's Reality*, Anne Wilson Schaef identifies an emerging female system in a white male society. She points out that men's psychological interpretation of women has often been incorrect because the men are working from their own male system – men's own perspective and experience – which is not the same as women's. For example, she would say to Freud that she has seldom met a woman who wished she had a penis, as he suggested in his theory of 'penis envy of women'; and to Erikson that the inner space he accurately observed in women is for babies only some of the time, and more usually for each woman to fill with her own being which empowers actions of herself and others.[1] Women's new awareness is of *not* being a weaker sex; is of *not* being in role always to 'mother' and patch up others, or of accepting the role of 'bad woman' such as bossy teacher.

On the other hand, the men in the above brief dialogues show a lack of awareness of the women's self-identity, and yet a certain uneasiness in themselves that leads them to reply as they do. They are conditioned by our western culture that has inherited patterns of philosophical thinking that define life experience by pairs of opposites. We are alive or dead, we are in heaven or on earth, we are male or female. When man defined woman, he described her as opposite and therefore other in relation to himself. Adrienne Rich points out in *Of Woman Born* that 'The dominant male culture, in separating man as knower from both woman and from nature as the objects of knowledge, evolved certain intellectual polarities which still have the power to blind our imaginations. Any deviance from a quality valued by that culture can be dismissed as negative.'[2] If man is strong, woman is weak; man is born of mother, women are to mother; women are to be weaker and caring, not strong with voices like school teachers! Most men have become aware that the old stereotypes no longer simply apply. Women's passion is acknowledged, but in a twisted way that tries to control by ridicule. Other stories illustrate the twists used unconsciously by men priests to keep control in their own power. A visiting priest says to a woman colleague, 'I insist that you do not use "men" in the liturgy.' He does not listen to her reasons for not yet changing parts of the liturgical language in that particular church, and apparently does not recognise that his dominating authoritarian manner is far more oppressive than the generic use of the word 'man'. A woman priest described her early celebrations of the eucharist as overshadowed by the heavy presence of her incumbent, who had suddenly become very 'chivalrously' attentive. It felt to her that he could not let go of 'his altar'. Or could it be that he is seeking a way to relate to her 'kite' energy, her creative energy that he has previously related to in a sexual stereotypical manner – he is man and she is woman?

Physical sex also may be acted out and 'explained' in terms of social conditioning 'A woman needs a man', 'she turned him on', 'he couldn't help himself', 'boys will be boys', are some inherited jargon phrases that cloud the truth of what really happens. We fail to declare that it is wrong for one human being to take what they want from another, or to assume that they know the needs of another. Masculine myths about the feminine are abundant. 'If he is a male professional and she is in his care, he can permit himself to believe that her erotic powers are so strong as to overwhelm his ability to make an ethical decision to refrain from having a sexual relationship with her.'[3] Women who are in touch with their own sexuality will challenge this myth. The priesthood now has in it women to challenge on behalf of all women, and to work with women whose experience they are close to. For 'Many forbidden-zone relationships fatally re-enact ... scenarios: a woman, closed down to herself but adapted to meet the expectations of others, puts hope and trust in a male therapist, teacher, pastor, or lawyer ... the woman ... numbly turn(s) over her body ... to his needs.'[4]

When the media coverage of sexual violence is so obvious, how can anyone think that it does not happen where they live? Each pastor may well ask why he or she has not been approached by a victim. 'The church is too pure to understand what happened to me,' complained one incest victim. 'The church can't talk about sex,' exclaimed another.

As women priests say 'no' to some of the situations in which they find themselves, and to some of the myths they face, they are in danger of developing a new set of stereotypes to replace the old: men must always leave women alone at the altar; women must always change to inclusive language regardless of the situation; women must never be weak; women must not be trapped into mothering; women must stand up for roles named 'bad' in the male system; women are responsible for changing sexual habits. This reactive redefining of what it is to be a woman may free women initially, but it is only a stage on the way to working as priests in communities of men and women concerned to have equal discipleship of human beings with many different gifts. Men can only discover new ways of relating when women themselves change. Men and women need to give each other respectful space as changes evolve. Women are vulnerable with their new roles and integrity. Men are vulnerable as they find new and positive expression of their masculinity.

### *A new naming of differences?*

'Come along, girls,' he said to a group of women priests. 'All right, boy,' they replied. He was not amused.

'I just mother them,' she said about her male priest colleagues. 'They do just as I want.'

'The "pieta" says it all for me,' he declared. 'Wounded man held by ideal Mother.'

'I work with women,' said a bishop. 'There is my sister – she doesn't have a clear moral sense; there's the crippled old lady – she can't leave her house; there is the pregnant single mother – she must just concentrate on motherhood.' And some women deacons awaiting priesting asked him, 'What about inviting women to discipleship, and not labelling them by their problems?'

'I want to jointly parent my children with my wife,' the young priest declared.

'Instead of visiting each committee, I have invited them to send representatives to meet with me,' she announced.

In each adult there is the image of the child they once were. This is useful to know, since we read in Matthew 18.3 that we are to become as little children if we are to enter the kingdom of heaven. The girl and the boy in each of us is to be owned. Conflict happens when we replace each other's adult, responsible maturity with the younger image. Men have long kept women small and helpless in men's eyes by calling them girls. Women have invited men into dependence on their motherly selves by calling them boys. It is a power game that is played out. Such a game does not value the other human being as a disciple of Christ. However, each disciple needs to own their inner child for themselves. When men can own with compassion the boy within, then male vulnerability can be owned and fathers will not give sons the perfectionist view of manhood that has been part of our inherited culture. Without the traditional pressure of expectations of success, status and sexual achievements, boy-children and young men will grow up more graciously and with less violence. As women's voices are heard speaking out against male perfectionist ideals, all human beings will be freer to be themselves and not rigorously trained into stereotypes. We do not need to deteriorate into chaos, but to know that we are acceptable human beings if we are 'good enough mothers', 'good enough husbands' etc. In *The Trouble with Boys*, Angela Philips writes,

> This book is not a recipe for better boys; it is an attempt to start untying the knot of masculinity and looking for the road signs that may help parents, and others concerned with young people, to mark out a new road for boys to follow, one that will allow them to recognize that they don't need to be better than girls in order to be men and that masculinity can be just as variable as feminity has become.[5]

Leadership of women priests encourages all women to be themselves and to question systems and stereotypes that have possibly prevented that. Men are invited to that freedom, too. Changes are happening. Deborah Holder writes in the *Guardian* (31 August 1994) that although the London Marriage Guidance Council saw almost three times as many women as men in 1993, 2,921 men had gone for counselling. This is a shift from the groove in which men say, 'I can't talk', and their partners say, 'He never talks to me.' The next few years will show fruits of women's priesting, depending on the churches' ability to relate to the community.

We are an 'Easter People', and within that understanding 'pieta' moves to waiting alone with God in the tomb, and then to resurrection. Women who refuse in all honesty to collude with fixed idealised images of woman bring healing for men and for other women who are held by rigid, limited models. Women's 'kite' energy lifts the spirits of us all to the Holy Spirit, and the exhausted mother no longer needs to hold her wounded son – she no longer needs her 'codeines'. The woman leader says 'Report to me, now we are established.' She no longer moves around to serve and nurture. She changes her mode of ministry at the appropriate time. Alternatively, where women have been seen as pastoral case-studies – objects with problems to solve – they can instead be named human beings called to discipleship. To live our truth is an essential part of developing healthy spirituality. Homosexual people forced by the church to hide their truth from themselves carry a dark repressed shadow out of which they can be very cruel – especially to women. To name differences of orientation would be healing for all people. The Right Reverend Derek Rawcliffe, when he 'came out' in March 1995, said, 'The priesthood as a whole is a haven – no, an attraction, for gay men. Gay men, on the whole, are more gentle and sensitive, and these are attributes that ought to belong to the priesthood . . . though some can be awful bitches.'

Clergy couples are particularly well placed to share parenting of children and to open up the concept for others. In a paper delivered by Martin Percy at a workshop on 'The Family', in Bedford on 17 September 1994, he pointed out that the Year of the Family calls Christians to look widely in the mess and the richness, and face up to the realities of human life, not to collude with secrecy and denial. As a priest married to a priest, he and Emma, living their family life among God's people, are challenging stereotypes and finding living realities of Covenant People here and now.

### Back to basics?

'When women are priests they can show us the family values of the Scriptures,' declared an ardent member of a church wives group.

'The Gospels describe equal discipleship for men and women,' states a feminist advocate of women priests.

'The woman priest must expect to carry her cross when some people do not want her ministry,' says a church-warden.

'Nature has no reason but to serve man and [science is] tinctured with orthodox Christian arrogance towards Nature', according to Lynn White, the American historian, in an attack on the Judaeo-Christian tradition. He is quoted by Jonathon Porritt in his essay 'Let the Green Spirit Live' (1990).

Which scriptural families shall we look at? Could they be the patriarchal tribal households of Abraham and others in the book of Genesis, or the city households of the Wisdom writings in the book of Proverbs, or the households of the Christian converts in the Graeco-Roman society of 1 Peter, or the family of the very early church in which marriage was not considered necessary, or the Holy Family? Is there a common thread to which we might refer, that links these families in their different cultures? All are in covenant with God and each other.

This covenant is expressed according to cultural understanding. In Genesis, we read of the patriarchs having several wives, of having sex with slave girls given to them by their wives to produce children. These people understood that their covenant with God was to be fruitful and multiply. A barren woman was not blessed by God. An alternative must be found. By the times of Solomon and onwards, women's gift for establishing well-being in households that are efficiently run and in which people are cared for is expressed as Wisdom in which God delights. The 'household codes' of 1 Peter are based on the 'household codes' of Aristotle and Plato, which order society into cities, households, and an order of dominance and submission within them. Wives are to obey husbands: within Christian understanding, this is explained in the theology of the cross. It is virtuous to submit, even to suffering, for the greater good. In the very early church marriage was not considered necessary because children were not necessary with the end-time of Christ's second coming imminent. The Holy Family is not idealised in scripture as it is in much of our inherited tradition. Joseph struggles with his covenanted relationship with God before marrying Mary, who is pregnant, but not by him. The boy Jesus is in conflict with his parents when he lingers in the Temple to learn of his covenant with God, and so on. If women priests make community of men and women equal in ways that work at our covenant with God in our society at this end of the twentieth century, then we shall go back to basics in a very real way. We shall not return to basics by trying to imitate customs of a God-covenanted people of a past age.

Do the Gospels describe equal discipleship of men and women? Four writers in *The Women's Bible Commentary*[6] argue that this is only partial. Amy-Jill Levine writes, 'While Matthew has not designed a community in which women and men have entirely equal roles, the Gospel recognizes the contributions made to the growth of the church by women as well as by others removed from positions of power (foreigners, lepers, the possessed, and the dispossessed).'[7] Mark's Gospel, Mary Ann Tolbert points out, has women in the position of receiving healing and teaching until chapters 15 and 16, when 'the central role of women in this final episode of the Gospel has raised the question of the importance of women throughout the narrative'.[8] 'The Gospel of Luke is an extremely dangerous text, perhaps the most dangerous in the Bible,' warns Jane Schaberg.[9] She goes on to explain that although Luke has many women in his Gospel, they are subjects of teaching and objects of healing in a male-dominated script. By the end, the women have paled into insignificance. It is in John's Gospel that women have significantly positive roles, argues Gail R. O'Day. 'This significance is evident both in the number of stories in which women appear and in the theological importance of those stories.'[10] Women in John's Gospel come to discipleship in their own right. They are involved in mission and remain strong in faith. Perhaps they are too good to be true. After all, no women in this Gospel need healing: only the men are healed. Is this not equal discipleship, either?

It is the church that bears schism and divisions within it. Individual women do not carry the load alone. In her article 'Church and family in the scriptures and early church', Rosemary Radford Ruether protests against the theology of voluntary victimisation that she discerns in 1 Peter, and she writes of that letter, 'The cross of Christ is no longer a symbol of truth and justice which enables the Christian to stand against an unjust world, but it has become an example of patient and unprotesting acceptance of unjust suffering.'[11] Women priests have to discern a theology that challenges this so-called virtue of women's suffering. Instead of focusing on suffering, we claim resurrection, too, and as the Easter People we are, we celebrate the eucharist, the feast of the Easter People. We are all challenged to ask, 'Which basics are we called to return to?' Perhaps we shall focus less on God creating man in his image to subdue the earth, and claim instead the covenant of Genesis 9, in which God gives Noah the sign of the rainbow to show he is in covenant with human beings and all living creatures – a shift to a Christian theology that presupposes God in relationship with all creation.

### *Delight in difference?*

The congregation giggled quietly, for the new woman priest had just invited them to confess and 'to keep God's commandments and live in love and peace with all men'. Her gender gave a new meaning to this invitation.

A bishop says, 'We welcome Josephine Bloggs, our new representative for the Decade of Women in Solidarity with Women.' A voice replies, 'No, Bishop, it's the Decade of Churches in Solidarity with Women.'

Men in a mixed clergy cell, that used to study books together, declare that they only want to discuss books sometimes as the women have shown them it is good to swop stories!

He calls everyone 'lovey': 'Peter, lovey', 'Jane, lovey'. We are all loved.

'Why is he a priest, and she a woman-priest?' the child asked.

'We call our new vicar "Father Ann".'

'I'll do that,' he said. 'No, we'll share,' she responded.

A woman and a man priest were working together. There was much energy between them. Their eyes met – the choice to become intimate or to keep their space was theirs. 'My train is this way,' she said. 'See you tomorrow,' he called. The tense moment passed.

Meaning changes as the voice, personality, gender of the leader changes. The generic 'men' becomes a joke of woman about man, in the old stereotypes, when it is heard by people who do not know about the generic nouns of Latin or Greek. On the other hand, those of us who are used to referring traditionally to all human beings as 'men' have traditionally grouped women together to care for each other in women's groups etc., for 'we men leaders' do not really understand women. Men must be careful for sexual reasons not to come too close to women. Now that we have women leaders, too, they can be close to women. However, some men and women are fearful of losing the security of traditional ways and consequently label women as 'Father'. And what about women's ministry to men? We have a lot to sort out. Still we have to work out how to include men *and* women, i.e., how to be church. Susan Cooper, one of the organisers of WATCH (Women And The Church), set up to monitor the status of women in the Diocese of London, is reported in the *Church Times* of 23 September 1994 as saying, 'However favourable men are to the idea of women priests, if they've been involved in the Church for a long time they have no experience of working with women as equals.'

Listening to stories of each other's experience begins to happen. We have heard much of women's vulnerability over the last fifteen years or so. Now is the time to listen to men's vulnerability, too. James Nelson suggests, as in his paper read at Newcastle on 22 September 1994 at the launch of *Theology and Sexuality*, that clergymen in our industrial, entrepreneurial society have not been counted as 'proper men'. They have worked in parishes among the women in the domestic setting. They are not of the world, the world of men. Women now work, even among women, in parishes. Where does this leave clergymen? Learning to share leadership; learning that control and domination do not create relationships that are mutually respectful and in turn creative because people are different; learning that power in Christ involves listening, dying to ego-needs, being prepared to be an interacting part of community and of the whole of creation. Women and men who work with colleagues can discover new ways of relating. Our society, which is becoming aware that sexual violence is evil, that women can be provoked into violence as well as men, and that mothers abuse children, needs a church that can practically involve itself with relationships and sexuality.

The dialogue of difference between men and women is partly about opposites such as justice and care. Traditionally men have been concerned with justice and women with care. This split was strong in the male leadership of the 'Enlightenment' age of the nineteenth and early twentieth centuries when logical thought and science were valued highly and feelings were to be kept hidden. Morals were to be taught and enforced by law. Benevolence resulted from thinking what it would be like for the other person, not listening to their experience. Carol Gilligan observes:

> As we have listened for centuries to the voices of men and the theories of development that their experience informs, so we have come more recently to notice not only the silence of women but the difficulty in hearing what they say when they speak. Yet in the different voice of women lies the truth of an ethic of

care, the tie between relationship and responsibility, the origins of aggression in the failure of connection.[12]

Dialogue from such different places makes both women and men vulnerable, yet we can delight in the richness and creative potential it brings. We may even celebrate our differences instead of merely tolerating them.

As we are all 'Loveys', we can become more confident about our differences. Yet psychologists show us that we in our western culture are increasingly damaged human beings. We often repress fears rather than work with them and now it is understood that we may dissociate ourselves from other people, society, moral responsibilities etc. because we feel the need to cut off. Susie Orbach, writing in the *Guardian* (13 May 1995), says we can only be freed when we can own we are helpless: 'The recognition of helplessness is one of the most difficult emotional states to assimilate. To accept helplessness, one usually requires the acceptance and validation of another.' She also makes the point (*Guardian*, 8 July 1995) that as primary relationships set patterns for much of our future behaviour, we need secure adults to rear children. A church that works to this end has good news to offer. When we value difference, we no longer have a 'woman's problem', only a church's problem of working out community of women and men. We delight that each human being called to discipleship finds self-respect, self-knowledge, a place in the plan of things, and becomes an inheritor with others of the faith. We live reconciliation in a real way.

As we challenge the old patriarchal ways and embody our spirituality and sexuality together we have good news for a world violently split by the old patterns of behaviour. 'Fathering' is redeemed and is no longer dominant. There is more true loving in relationships and intimacies. Peter

Rutter writes, 'Because so many women have been previously injured by the uncontained sexuality of men who have had power over them, the potential healing power of restraint is enormous.'[13] The woman keeps her own inner energies for creative use, which may be for sexual expression or not, as she chooses. The man knows he is not driven, and has the ability to be restrained and tender. Spiritually men and women share Life, as glimpsed through Jesus the Way, Life that still rises from deathly experience. Only in Christ's Spirit can the differences, attractions and aching voids of our relationships weave the texture of our individual and corporate lives. The church learns as it lives into the gospel in each generation. Now, in the community of God's people, the priesthood of all the baptised is served by priests who are as different as the people themselves, and free to challenge the old systems and stereotypes – freer of codeines, and more integrated with kites!

## Notes

1 Anne Wilson-Schaef, *Women's Reality* (HarperSanFrancisco, 1981), pp. 33, 34.
2 Adrienne Rich, *Of Woman Born* (Virago, 1977), p. 62.
3 Peter Rutter, *Sex in the Forbidden Zone* (Unwin, 1990), p. 67.
4 Rutter, *Sex in the Forbidden Zone*, p. 79.
5 Angela Philips, *The Trouble with Boys* (Pandora, 1993), p. 16.
6 Carol A. Newsom and Sharon H. Ringe (eds), *The Women's Bible Commentary* (SPCK and Westminster/John Knox Press, 1992).
7 Amy-Jill Levine, 'Matthew' in *The Women's Bible Commentary*, p. 253.
8 Mary Ann Tolbert, 'Mark' in *The Women's Bible Commentary*, p. 263.
9 Jane Schaberg, 'Luke' in *The Women's Bible Commentary*, p. 275.
10 Gail R. O'Day, 'John' in *The Women's Bible Commentary*, p. 294.
11 Rosemary Radford Ruether, 'Church and family in the early church' in *New Blackfriars* (1984), p. 13.

12 Carol Gilligan, *In a Different Voice* (HarperSanFrancisco, 1982), p. 173.
13 Rutter, *Sex in the Forbidden Zone*, p. 215.

# 5   *A different way of working:*

*What women bring to collaborative ministry*

PENNY MARTIN

---

### Setting the scene

We sat in a circle. She was a canon, he was a bishop. She was a rural dean (and so was he!), several of us were wearing clerical collars, many had secular jobs, we were paid and unpaid, we worked part-time, full-time, overtime and often in time.

The meeting was nearing its close. There was a star-shaped exchange of dialogue across the circle:

'Who is going to give us the blessing?'

'I've brought one.'

'Will you read it?'

'Why don't you?'

'Let us pray . . .'

This is simply one example of the everyday, natural and enjoyable parts of working together, women and men, lay and ordained, which the changing pattern of ministry today is making possible. It is sharing the experience, the task, the problem, the joke, the solution and the reward, which brings the satisfaction, the frustration and sometimes the heartache of collaborative ministry. It is this element of balance and fullness that the ordination of women in the Church of England has opened up for us. Perhaps it comes from daughters and mothers very early

© 1996 Penny Martin

on, and again when daughters become mothers; a non-hierarchical way of tackling and solving the problem which is unselfconscious, just the way that women work and bring their way of working naturally to mixed groups.

## *The promise: part of a journey*

I have never worked alone. Even where I carried independent, autonomous responsibility, I have always sought, and been sought out, for the comparing of notes, the reflection of ideas, the evaluation of decisions. It could have something to do with being one of three sisters – 'What do you think about this?', 'Can you help me get hold of this?' – accommodating, smoothing out, compromising, finding a way through. Confronting, compensating for imbalance, above all a holding and a letting go.

When I came to a crossroads quite late on, women and men gave me encouragement to explore the path which eventually led to ordination. It was never clear to me more than a few steps at a time; one door opened, only to reveal the next. Almost from the very beginning, I have seen my path as a realisation and a promise. The realisation has taken hold of images and pictures which have always meant a great deal – I found myself drawn almost instinctively to the perspective of movement I have loved: places and spaces which beckoned me on in my mind and spirit; an open gateway, a turn in the road, a door left ajar. The promise is still, and has been, the next corner, the other side of the wall, the castle in the distance.

The invitation, that willingness to risk and fail, has been to go at my own pace, simply putting one foot in front of another, often dawdling while others overtook, or occasionally a breathless hurtle, swept along by the momentum of an urgent spirit.

Now I am in parish ministry, but since I was first

ordained as a deaconess in September 1986, I have never worked by myself. In a sense, we never do, because our ministry is always shared with other people; but the difference that women are now pioneering is that men and women can now experience more mutuality in our working together. I started out in parish ministry with two priests, one older and one younger than I was, but both affirming my own vocation to priesthood. Next, I worked in a chaplaincy team, and then for a short time with a non-stipendiary priest in poor health. His place was eventually taken by a man who was, and remains, bitterly opposed to women priests. We still managed to work together quite creatively, although at some personal cost. All along, there has been working alongside interested and involved lay people.

I think I am inclined to take issue with the term 'collaboration', as it is being applied to men and women in ministry together. In my present position, a plurality of three parishes, I share the pastoral and priestly responsibilities with two men, both younger than I am, and all of us have other areas of formal and informal ministry which take up some of our individual time.

Three priests, three parishes, a free association of gifts and ministries – not 'one man, one patch'. We each offer our best abilities, where they are needed, and we each take what we need from our combined resources.

We essentially 'work' together very little! With three churches and congregations, we could quite easily report and communicate at our weekly staff meeting, and otherwise go our own ways. We are finding that it is infinitely worth while to invest the extra time so that we can actually share our eucharistic and pastoral ministries, making opportunities to overlap and spend time together, as men and women, in worship, planning, reviewing, visiting, relaxing and especially in our celebration of Holy Communion.

Having had the unique experience of preparing with a special cohort of women for the first priestly ordinations, I have much valued the time to reflect on our ministry and priesthood. This has been greatly enriched by being able to test out many of the ideas and insights with my two colleagues, and to benefit from their (not always totally straightfaced!) responses. I have made great strides in learning how to be teased, and how to tease back.

So, rather than be defined by the term, 'collaborative ministry', I would like to think and write about *complementary priesthood* or – even more appealingly – what it means to be ordained ministers together. I look forward to developing a theme of *co-ordination*.

For me, then, the journey towards priesthood has been an emergence into an open space, sometimes bewildering and perplexing, but never in isolation. It has been an unfolding pathway, with other people as signposts and milestones, reference points, stepping stones and stumbling blocks. Now, occupying the space which God has opened out for us in the church, we could almost call ourselves 'Spacewomen' for we inhabit the interval of experience which has been awaiting our full contribution to the body-shape of Christ-people.

The more we think about the 'body' language we are invited to use and express in our Christian living, the more we warm to the concept of co-ordination.

## *Just like a woman?*

The perennial question is often, 'Is there a specifically feminine way of going about the task?' Part of the answer seems to become clearer in my bones as I continue to collect experience of learning with groups of women, with groups of men, and with mixed groups. There is a different way of tackling a learning project if there are women in the group: this is about the way I present my material, it figures in the early formation of the dynamics of the group, and it suggests the way I can offer myself to those whose interest and attention I am chasing.

Over the last eight years I have struggled with the puzzling and often painful issues which huddle around the subject of HIV-related illness and AIDS. At the beginning, I was usually in a predominantly male learning group (of the more enlightened variety), and it was mostly men who were doing the consciousness-raising. I learned to look some of my deepest fears in the eye, and to lift the corner of some of the most scary pages any of us are faced with; I peered tremulously at the meaning of my mortality. I explored the feel and the implications of my own sexuality and the excitements and taboos of how that interacts with the sexuality of others. I stopped to cherish the awareness of the things I love and live, and the potential pain of the loss of those same things.

Enduringly grateful for the depth and colour this learning gave and continues to give to the theology and meaning of my own living, I began to be involved in wider groups, still working with HIV and AIDS, but on the side of the facilitator as well as the learner. Interestingly, they were at first mainly groups of women – the caring professions, counsellors, youth leaders, church circles such as the Mothers' Union. One or two men would be among them, but I was preparing and presenting my material mostly for small, co-operating circles of women. Later I had to run the gauntlet of the dreaded chapter meeting: local clergy gathered for their monthly dose of worship, fraternising, business agenda (equals gossip) and the feature slot – me! In the beginning, these chapters were predominantly male and I found the prospect intimidating: going into a strange room, fifteen or so men often dressed in black, who all knew one another and not me, and – what a nerve! – I was asking them please to take a look at their fears about death, bereavement and sexuality.

What I came to learn was that the male group and the female group were not so very different on the inside, where these raw and real issues connected with their own sense of personhood; but the difference lay in how they handled the material, how they received it and worked with it. And I learned from the women in the beginning how to be comfortable myself and how to put them at their ease. With this skill at least sometimes at my fingertips, I found I could be more true to myself with the men, and although they reacted differently, I could still make it safe enough for them to look at some of the difficult things I wanted them to touch on.

An initial sharing of myself has to be at least partly sprinkled with humour, otherwise it would be far too serious to invite others into. We can use the sometimes loaded phrases and sexist patterns to our advantage, if we can resist being too offended by them. That way, we gain control of them. 'Just like a woman'? 'A woman's place'? 'Women's work'? These titles are quivering with potential if we use them as springboards and respond to them with a sense of fun. And once I found how to capitalise with them in a female group, I dared to use them with the men.

Part of our rambling and richly-peopled summer holidays has sometimes consisted of mixed ability and varied levels of enthusiasm over bicycle rides. Once, twenty-five of us planned a day out on our motley collection of racers, hired rattlers and serious cross-country specimens. A huge and unwieldy picnic was shared among the panniers, the saddlebags and the haversacks. We left the planning of the route to the men and the boys while the women reflected on the coming demands of the day ahead.

With some trepidation I committed myself to my comfortable saddle but resisted the implication that I should be responsible for the first-aid kit, the puncture kit, the water sterilisation tablets. I rapturously announced I had all I needed; a drink of water, a lipstick and a change of earrings. This silenced all anxiety in me and in them. We had a lovely day.

What I want to draw from this story is that I have used it over and over again as an introduction to a self-valuing exercise. What would I take with me if the house burned down, the hurricane threatened, the end of the world was at hand? What have I already in my personal resources? Being able to be 'just like a woman' but with the humour and acceptance that a woman can so often bring. A genuine and creative aspect of groups, whether of men or women, or mixed, is that we learn to take the risk of not being too serious about ourselves, while taking one another seriously.

It is a rewarding exercise to observe the way in which systems of people operate, and particularly in the context of shared ministry, to see some of the specific patterns in which women co-operate in a predominantly female work environment. I use this as an excuse to spend a little longer at the hairdressers, or to make good use of the waiting time in a supermarket queue or the outpatients' department; on the whole the level of competitiveness between women who work together is notably less than between men. We are not nearly so afraid to share a mistake or a self-doubt with another woman. 'I can't see how to get this to work'; 'Have you any idea where I can find this piece of information?'; 'That wasn't all that brilliant, was it? I'll know next time.'

In my experience, once a team of ministers begins to

relax enough to enjoy one another, the feminine element of sharing resources, personal and professional, becomes a rewarding contribution to the way women and men live and reflect the gospel.

## Gathering for change

As women who had waited for so long for the opening to us of the ordained priesthood, we had understandably formed, by the time the legislation happened, strong bonds and shared resources for collaborative ministry. One of my (male) colleagues describes it, as we still thank God for it, as a 'sacrament of waiting'. The gift of this unchosen, sometimes frustrating and very often painful waiting time was that for the first time, groups of ordained women came together to prepare for the birth of their priestly ministry.

In the Diocese of Durham over a two-year period, we were able to gather together on several precious occasions, to reflect on our theology of ministry and priesthood, and to combine this with shared experience and the opportunity to identify and explore some of our expectations, and other people's. The all-woman texture of these gatherings often felt over-feminised. Women together can of course be irritating and lack the snap and crackle of mixed groups, with their subliminal sexual chemistry. I often used to think that an all-female priesthood would be at least as problematic as an all-male one.

But far beyond the minor disadvantages of not having any men around, we grew together as Christian women, as Anglican ministers, as friends and associates through these waiting days. As the trust grew, we learned to share, with tears of humour and frustration, the last stages of the journey. We were able to take stock of the ways we had come, which had covered a wide landscape of life-experience and ministerial history. Our ages ranged from women on the edge of retirement, to very newly emerged deacons. We were of all Anglican persuasions, of mixed liturgical and pastoral traditions; yet waiting together in faith we found and strengthened our resolve, our confidence. We shared our journeys to vocation, listened with a sense of privilege and prayer to the call and story we each brought. We were quiet, we were uproarious; we sang quietly to God, we stamped our feet; but I for one will always be deeply grateful for the opportunity to unfold the map of my priestly journey in the company of other women with different maps but the same journey; we folded and re-folded them again, but with clearer perspectives and a greater sense of destiny as our ordination day was named and as we saw our way, not only to the day itself but through and beyond to all the promise of the future for women and men as priests together.

We were women in waiting. As women, waiting seems to be part of our calling in life. As women have done all down the ages, we wait for the times to be born, and we wait for the times of dying. We often do this together, gathered round the birthing and the dying of those whom we love and support. Almost always, the actual moment we are waiting for is out of our hands. Attending to a birth or a death, we realise the profoundness of life; in the event, we can do little to hasten or to slow either process, we cannot entirely choose the timing or the circumstances of its happening. We simply wait, and do so with our sisters if we have them near us.

As we gathered for change, women in waiting, we thanked God together for the ways we had come, even with so much pain and struggle. The pain and the struggle in themselves became a precious element of the lives and ministries we were offering back to God. This was not just the pain and struggle of the women, but of all those who had felt it and wrestled with it. On one occasion, just before the final Synod decision, someone remarked to me that I was wearing the colours of the suffragettes: purple, green and white. I had not been conscious of the connection, but afterwards I felt an added link with those other women in waiting. I still do, as the purple stole of Advent-Lent and the green of all those ordinary Sundays is unfolded over the white alb or surplice.

It was on this same day that I found the promise of God that the day would come. We had gathered, men and women, all ages and colours and backgrounds, to be together and to worship in Coventry Cathedral. The Movement for the Ordination of Women had arranged the service to claim the promise, 'Christ before us'. I remember the music and the dancer who weaved his coloured streamer in and out of the congregation. The moment I believed it would happen was when we turned to leave the new Cathedral – the colourful procession moved back through the people and into brilliant, almost unbearably bright sunshine, streaming in through the high glass doors. Emerging into the light, men and women together, robed and anorak-ed, we still waited and worked together for the promise, but I knew it would be kept. Collaborative ministry is about more than the doing, it is surely about the waiting, the wanting and the moment of faith.

## *Language!*

Speech is as much a bodily function as anything. Once we articulate an idea or a feeling – a hope, a fear, a desire, a dread – we give it a shape, a tangible reality which may not have been there before. Others may now identify something which was personal and private before we spoke it. We cannot unsay it, however much we may wish to try. Particularly in our worship and in our 'God-speak', we are voicing the deepest and holiest thoughts and longings, giving form and body to the transcendent. So it is not surprising that language has become a live issue in the worshipping and witnessing of our everyday Christian ministries. It follows that where women and men are able to share the formation and the saying-out of our liturgies, it matters more than we often realise how we go about it.

The raisers of consciousness have never undertaken a comfortable task. In order to learn the ways in which some of our language causes sections of humanity to feel excluded and unwelcome, we first have to feel that exclusion and discomfort. This is perhaps why the first forays into inclusive language, in whatever context, cause such currents of anger and resentment before they bear fruit.

Where there is growing experience of shared ministry between laypeople and ordained worship leaders, men and women, younger and older members of congregations, the necessary discomforts of tidying up the exclusiveness of our liturgical language can be lightened by the humour and common sense that such collaboration makes possible. There are ridiculousnesses about the correct personal pronoun, just as there are glaring offences in the careless talk of exclusively worded prayers and liturgies.

However, it is our experience that only now that we have the opportunity merely to raise the point, or to demonstrate by considerate example, ministers who find their voice together in the expression of theology and prayer have a rewarding and even enjoyable time as they pick their way through the minefields of inclusive language. Simply by standing side by side in front of a congregation, a man and a woman ministering together highlight the difficulty; but much more constructively, we can then go on to offer solutions to the problem. We find the work of pointing out the mistake is uncomfortable and causes discomfort; but the joy of it is that we can go on in the balance of shared ministry to put the matter right, to lighten the atmosphere when it becomes overladen, and to celebrate the completeness of liturgy when the offence is overcome.

In the mixed ministerial teamwork where I have made my mistakes and learned to be considerate with inclusive language, I have had the most enormous fun. It is difficult to harbour resentment or feel affronted when your colleague is singing away about 'Good News to men in all the earth', and you are wearing an expression of blissful innocence, while standing very firmly on his foot!

The healthy exchanges of open teamwork and loyal, supportive collaborations yield rich rewards in the discovery, development and demonstration of equality in our ministering, whether that be in public worship or in a more personal pastoral setting. I have found that simply having a woman in on the conversation has often been enough to see that words are more carefully chosen. Many times the banter has escalated into quite outrageous proportions, but the good nature of an enjoyable working relationship has rarely left us nursing any lasting damage. I am thankful that in the language of our everyday communication we are able to demonstrate quite naturally the value that we recognise in one another.

In this way, a team of ministers, and particularly a mixed team, has a gift to offer to worshipping congregations and to everyday conversationalists, the sign and sacrament of truly being included in the love of God.

## Embodiment and metaphor

As someone who listens and talks for a living (among other things, and including prayer in this category), I have come to realise about myself that I naturally process my thoughts, whether in creative thinking or in making sense of the world I experience, in mind-pictures. There is a school of counselling technique known as the Healing Metaphor, where the client is encouraged to locate the difficulty somewhere in a bodily sensation: 'like a band round my head', 'like a lump in my throat', 'it feels like a great load on my shoulders'. It is a skilled and delicate process, but the trained counsellor can sometimes use an offered metaphor to develop and follow through the client's past experiences of hurt or self-protection, and come out into the open place of healing. In appreciating this specialised counselling 'tool', I note two peripheral factors: one is that I instinctively use metaphor, thought-pictures and visualisation in counselling, as I listen and retain the client's story. The other factor is that as I offer to the client possible ways of exploring the subject, I find myself offering the option of a metaphor: 'Is it like this?'; 'Can you give it any kind of shape or colour?' As always, the clients instinctively choose which offer they wish to take up, and whether they actually do so. In my experience, though I hesitate to make a generalization, more women than men respond to metaphorical suggestion and go on to appreciate it in their language of growth.

There is a rapport, then, when my own pictorial thought-process connects with someone else who thinks in the same way, and this particular element becomes a creative and colourful strand in our communication. Men and women who are open to the metaphorical or visionary way of thinking are usually more ready to recognise the embodiment of much of Christian theology, and are likely to be excited about the sensation of their faith-experience and to share that of other people.

The fact that Jesus was the physical expression of God's love and forgiveness therefore has a special appeal in the metaphorical thinker. Just preferring to picture the gospel narratives, to respond easily to the story style of the parables – 'It was like this – a man went to sow a field' – brings faith to life. Jesus, carried in Mary's body and born of it, growing up and grazing his knee, having his voice break and his beard grow, walking till his feet ached and enjoying food and wine – this Jesus is real and close, this Jesus stretched out his arms for us on the cross. This Jesus had a body which did not stay dead.

As our faith and salvation is embodied in Jesus Christ, so our response to the delights and struggles of everyday life, and the effort to make sense of it all in the light of what we believe, can be embodied in metaphor. This is not helpful to everyone, but if like me you recognise that you think in pictures, then we travel our faith-journey together.

In terms of collaborative ministry, I became more aware than ever of metaphorical rapport during the painful and lengthy journey towards the priesting of women. I have described earlier the valuable opportunity we had as deacons preparing for priesthood to explore and share our vocational experience. Not long before the final vote in General Synod, we had such a gathering on a quiet morning and sat round reflecting and praying about change, uncertainty and transitional fear. One of the deacons was pregnant and not far from term. She had waited long and at one stage had lost hope that she and her husband could give birth to a child of their own. The pregnancy was experienced as a daily miracle, and everyone knew the delivery would be tricky, just as they knew the child was especially precious.

She told us that day that she had a date to go into hospital, and that the morning after, she would have a caesarian section. We prayed for them and I went away with her on my mind. In my own prospect of the approaching synod vote, I came to identify the decision with Caroline's baby.

I was a voting member of the synod, though a very new one. With so many months and years of longing and waiting and praying behind us, we now knew the exact day and time of the decision, but there was no way of knowing what the outcome would be – just as Caroline knew the date and time of her baby's birth, and just as she could not know whether or not her baby would live.

The point of this story is that I found in the metaphor of Caroline's baby a way of anticipating the uncertainty of the synod decision, and more importantly, a way of communicating it to other people. The published proceedings of General Synod on 11 November 1992 record that in the final debate, I made my maiden speech and that later that afternoon, the child was born alive. The metaphor was taken up by many. In a healing eucharist on the evening of that day, I sat with a woman who had voted against, though she had agonised over the decision. We talked afterwards, and she said she was relieved the uncertainty was over, and believed that we would come to a wholeness of ministry. We reflected, the baby had arrived, but it looked like being a troublesome child . . .

So often, in the important and life-changing stages of our struggle to make sense of our lives in the light of our Christian faith, it is the familiar metaphor of our own bodies which helps us most. The New Testament is full of such body language: especially of course in the Pauline metaphor of the church as the body of Christ. 'If one part of the body suffers, all the other parts suffer with it; if one part is praised, all the other parts share in its happiness.

All of you are Christ's body, and each one is a part of it' (1 Corinthians 12.26 and 27, Good News Bible); and 'There is one body and one spirit, just as there is one hope to which God has called you'; 'the whole body grows and builds itself up through love' (Ephesians 4.4 and 16b).

Working naturally with picture language and metaphor, it has followed for me that the body illustration has been very creative. In the development of priesthood and ministry with my colleagues and with others with a perhaps less formal ministry, the embodiment of Christ in individual Christians, and the growth and movement of the church as a whole, continues to teach me new truths about being faith-people together.

### 'Co-ordination'

On 11 November 1992 the Synod voted, and with all the strain of waiting and the anguish of uncertainty, the child was born. Thanks be to God, the child was alive, but it was a difficult birth, as we had known it would be, accompanied by fear and partition and other people's pain. As the midwives of the legislation, our job was far from over, for midwives have to stay around to tidy up the mess. The days following the vote until the day of priesting itself seemed to me very much like the days following a birth. Have you noticed how a newly delivered mother spends hours simply looking at her child? All through the long months, they have a developing relationship; the mother knows her unborn child, they become intimately close, emotionally involved, mutually aware of one another's slightest movement. But not until the birth can the mother actually see her child. Then she just wants to look and look, and the child gazes back at her.

The church ordained me to the priesthood, with the

other women of the Durham Diocese, on 29 May 1994. To me, those first days after the ordination were very like the first days of wonder and realisation following a birth. Soon afterwards, I wrote these words:

### First days

*Lilac time;*
*purple, white and green,*
*a priest is born.*
*Colours of the waiting years,*
*and after all the weeks,*
*full term,*
*the sacrament of waiting over now,*
*emerging from this priestly womb*
*I see your face.*
*Familiar, yet till now unseen,*
*we look and look. With level eyes,*
*the child and bearer recognise.*
*In cradle weeks*
*we could well find*
*in water, oil, in wine and bread,*
*the new-born child*
*rocks you in priestly arms.*
*Together bring*
*God's life into the world.*

So now, the reality was here. Many aspects of ministry were just the same as before: the people, the parish, the everyday round of worship and activity. But I was changed, and more importantly, the church had changed. We would indeed never be the same again; and this was right and good. Collaborative ministry did not, of course, begin here. But priestly partnership did. I was now occupying the space which had been waiting for me, and the reality held a sense of rightness and companionability which simply fell into step with the priestly ministry of my colleagues and the shared faith-world of the people and the community to whom we were ministering.

The body metaphor continues to enlighten and to define the reality of the experience of being a priest, and being a priestly partner. Hands became expressive of the celebration which they now enacted. I could now realise how shared ministry was infinitely more balanced and functional than isolated ministry – what I had known with my head I could now handle and hold. When we use our hands, we employ a natural team of juxtaposition, which functions in creative tension one with one another; holding and releasing, knowing the sensations of pressure and relaxation. The wholeness of the combined function involves movement, support, stress, comfortableness, warmth, growth, grace, mutuality and interdependence. We take for granted the ease with which we wash our hands – running the water, lathering the soap, rinsing and drying. But try this with one hand behind your back, or with an armful of wriggling toddler, and you realise how much one hand needs the other!

The idea of 'collaboration' was actually *being* members together of the body of Christ. As priests and people together, we form a living expression of the interdependence, the balanced function, of God's life and commitment to the world we inhabit. Co-operative ministry is not just about 'collaboration', about working together, but about existing as parts of a body in which balance, give and take, activity and relaxation, ease and discomfort all contribute to the practicality of living out our Christian lives. This is why I prefer to think of it as 'co-ordination', in the sense that the parts of our bodies are co-ordinated and function together to walk or run, to dance or to carry a load. As co-ordained ministers, priestly and lay, we actually become the expression of the bodiliness, the incarnation of God's life in the world.

Over the time that these words have been being written, there has been much change in the ministry pattern of which I form a part. The change has been unexpected, unwelcome and painful to manage, with one member moving on, and the whole shape of the team disrupted and disorganised. The members of the clergy have regrouped and we continue to enjoy a good and creative relationship, but the lessons for each of us and for the parish are being learned with vulnerability and uncertainty.

During this time, it became almost impossible to write about collaborative ministry, or co-ordination. While the body felt as if it was disintegrating, all the members could do was to support and strengthen one another for the continuing pastoral and priestly ministry of our place. Now the transition is being achieved and the future shape is emerging; now that there is new direction and promise, we can see so much more clearly that the difficult way we have travelled was the path to a new and different ministry pattern; please God, even a better one. But nothing good is ever wasted.

There was to be a lesson I had not expected to learn when this chapter was conceived; and the lesson is completely consistent with the embodied theology of co-ordination about which I have been writing. Change is uncomfortable and involves loss and grieving, in ministry situations just as in the experience of our physical bodies. I sprain my ankle, I swell and bruise, I lose my balance and need support. I limp and hop, but eventually I can put my foot to the ground again and trust it not to hurt.

Through the experience of our changing ministry pattern, my co-ordained friends and I are now discovering new and untapped resources of lay ministry in the parishes, which have no doubt always been there, but which are finding the confidence to respond to our altered situation. Gifts are being offered, love and support are more apparent than ever, we are learning to rely more on one another, to ask for what we need, and to share the skills and knowledge that we have perhaps kept to ourselves. The body is looking further, reaching outwards and offering more open arms.

## *Incarnation*

Nothing good is ever wasted. I continue to discover, in joy and in pain, the living, growing reality of shared, priestly ministry. We are co-ordained in a body which flourishes with the realisation of the wholeness of women and men, in formal orders and in lay gifts.

I see the birth-day of 29 May 1994 as the release-moment for all of this. Picture Durham Cathedral on Trinity Sunday morning. Later that day, in the eleventh-century beauty of St Laurence, Hallgarth, there would be a celebration of the eucharist among the parish people. It was to be the most natural experience in the world. I wrote some other words then, which hold and then release all that I have tried to say here:

### *Ordination: Trinity Sunday, Durham Cathedral*

> . . . *after the waiting, minutes crawl*
> *until the bells peal and we stand*
> *in the cool air of the cloister, ready to*
> *join the swing of the procession.*
> *Welcome faces smile, encourage;*
> *lilac flowers white crowd the stony ledge.*
> *And unseen weight of hands my head bears.*

*From the quiet, morning-early two at prayer,*
*to Cuthbert splendour and*
*Laurence light of evening,*
*God is here.*
*Touching in my body,*
*breathing in my air,*
*living in my hands;*
*born powerfully within me,*
*brings me new alive,*
*aware and vulnerable,*
*I pain and dance in one joy-swell.*

*What is this that you have breathed*
  *into my ready heart?*
*What is this that you have gifted*
  *into my open hands?*
*Christ-words in a woman voice,*
*man-woman in an icon share.*
*This is my body, this my life,*
*O Breath of God, you all but sweep away*
        *this new priest.*

# 6  Being realistic about feminism
BARBARA BAISLEY

## Casablanca – the dilemma

*Casablanca* was recently voted the most popular film of all time – even those few who have never seen it know the catch-phrases: 'Play it again Sam', instantly recognisable, although never said in the film, and 'Here's looking at you, kid' and the wonderful Dooley Williams version of 'As time goes by'. It is pure romantic fantasy, just right for a wet, lazy, November afternoon.

On just such a day, a year or two ago, I was happily immersed, a pile of half-written Christmas cards beside me assuaging my guilty sense of self-indulgence. Ilse (Ingrid Bergman) was back with Rick (Humphrey Bogart) and had just declared she would not have the strength to leave him again. Bogart asks 'What about Lazlo?' (her freedom-fighter, hero, husband) and Bergman, tossing her head on his shoulder in agony declares, 'I can't fight it any more', then, 'Oh, I don't know what's right any more! You have to think for both of us, for all of us.' Her head nestles into his neck, she smiles 'tremulously', tears glistening on her lashes – 'You bitch,' I found myself thinking, the emotional spell shattered, 'you've just dumped it all on him.'

My reaction startled me to such an extent that the film's final climactic minutes were quite lost on me. I realised that something had been broken for me, had changed in me, without my being aware of it. Not only Ingrid

© 1996 Barbara Baisley

Bergman, but all those beautiful, innocent, childlike figures that had formed my image of ideal womanhood were suddenly exposed as just that, 'childlike'. They no longer fitted my idea of relationships between the sexes, and I no longer aspired to share their experience. This was no sudden change, and of course I would always have claimed to have been fully aware of the silver screen reflecting fantasy rather than reality. But I had not realised how far I had journeyed, or that I had lost something on the way, and I was not sure how I felt about the exchange.

That afternoon's viewing left me wondering about the significance of that 'ideal', repeated and reflected back so pervasively and persuasively, from Jane Austen to *The Taming of the Shrew*, from Jane Eyre to Scarlett O'Hara. The endlessly repeated message, that what women *really* want and need is to find a man strong enough, physically, mentally and emotionally, to allow them to retreat into childhood with a 'You think for both of us', as they lean confidingly against his manly chest. Despite our experience to the contrary, despite our achievements, the majority of women still act out patterns of social behaviour modelled on that premise, if not expecting doors to be opened, chairs pulled back, tyres pumped, deferring to men in conversation, glancing up from under the lowered eyelids, understanding 'instinctively' that the best way to gain our ends is to bend a little, flatter a little and smile, smile, smile. Much fear of feminism, from both sexes, is an often unconscious unease about how to conduct relationships if the old rules no longer to apply, and how to think about ourselves and our identity as men and women. How to be a man, if the strong hero protecting women from the rough and wicked world is no longer required; as a woman, how to relate to men without manipulating them, flirting with them, and always, endlessly, trying to please.

True, *Casablanca* was made over fifty years ago, true, it reflected myth rather than reality, but myths are both powerful and durable. The questions remain: do we want to move on, how do we keep some sort of balance in the new world we are making, what wisdom can the church find that might offer hope?

## My own journey

Although I was aware from an early age of my ambivalence about 'being a girl', it has taken me much longer to understand the contradictory nature of the messages I received.

Born in the post-war baby-boom years, I was the late and last born child of a quiet, gentle and scholarly father and a strong-willed mother who had hoped she had completed her family, with a neat 'boy and a girl' in the early years of the war.

My mother was a woman of vision, who passionately believed that her own fulfilment and purpose in life were to be an inspiration to her children. She 'taught' constantly, talking to us about her childhood experiences, her girlhood in France and Germany, and her own convictions. As the youngest, by several years, I was very much her confidante as a young child, uncritically absorbing all she had to say. She instilled in me a sense of the possibilities of life, insisting that if I only had access to books, I could achieve anything I set my mind on – 'This is all yours,' she would declaim, on a visit to the British Museum or National Gallery. 'It is *kept* here so everyone can see it, but it belongs to the nation, that means it belongs to you!' It felt wonderful. She also had clear ideas about the different natures of the sexes, which totally contradicted her own character, but which instilled in me the belief that boys were dominant, lively, articulate, straightforward, and active, whereas girls were, or should be, quiet, shy, naturally submissive, manipulative, dishonest, 'sexual' and less intelligent than their brothers. I remember being commended for 'taking it like a boy', when one of her frequent eruptions of anger resulted in a swift slap. This was in contrast to my sister, whom my mother reported to be 'slippery' – I imagine that meant she was quick enough to avoid the soapy hand emerging from the dish-water.

However, at the same time as holding this parody of male and female stereotypes, my mother gloried in motherhood as a vocation and held it up as superior to any other calling or career for man or woman. She believed in women being well educated in order that they might 'educate their children', and painted vividly romantic pictures of the supreme joy and satisfaction of pregnancy, giving birth and mothering small children, quite at variance with her evident frustration and physical exhaustion. The strongest message was that 'boys were best' and I longed to be a boy, dreamed of being a boy, played at being a boy, but always with the knowledge that I wanted to grow up to be a woman in order to be able to become a 'mother'.

As if these confusions were not enough, at the age of seven I was sent to an independent girls' school with a strong and proud tradition. Year by year I would hear the Founder's Day Address, telling me of Miss Buss who founded the school in 1850 in order that girls might enjoy the same education as their brothers. I drank in the 'saving history' of her determination that the curriculum should include maths and Latin as did boys' schools, of the struggle for girls to sit public examinations and go on to higher education and careers on the same terms as boys and young men. But true to the earlier inculcation of my mother, I balked at the challenge of 'You girls will be able to have careers *and* a family'. I only intended a short-term career, to be superseded by the sweetness of romance and the 'greater calling' of motherhood.

I know that I am far from alone in having received such contradictory messages – boys are good, girls are less good; girls are just as good as boys; girls have a right to the same education as boys; girls' education is primarily to make them good mothers; it is 'better' to be at home than out at work; men are active, women are passive – while often our nurturing experience is of an active mother and a passive or largely absent father. Countless women recount similar experiences and similar confusion and self-rejection. Perhaps the definition of original sin being 'centred on self', needs a modification clause: 'NB: for women the fundamental sin is not knowing who their self is'. Re-examining psychological theory in the light of women's experience, Jean Baker Miller writes:

> The concept of the self has been prominent in psychological theory, perhaps because it has been one of the central ideas in Western thought ... As we have inherited it, the notion of 'self' does not appear to fit women's experience ... A question then arises: Do only men, and not women, have a self?[1]

For years I tried to work out my identity in accordance with the messages I had received, wanting to be accepted as a 'proper' woman, while despising the feminine and knowing myself to be not at all domesticated, quiet or submissive. After marriage and almost immediate parenthood, I became a member of a church, mixing in 'fellowship groups' with women of all ages. There was a strong sense of comradeship and support, much of the conversation reinforcing the notion that men were intrinsically different: 'They wouldn't understand, of course'; 'Well, what do you expect from a man!' There was an assumption that women's 'knowledge' was of a different order to men's, and that although men saw themselves as superior, we knew better. While I enjoyed the sense of solidarity and inclusion, I also began to observe a common pattern of depression amongst many of the women whose families had grown up and who had underachieved academically early in life and now felt trapped in the home, with little purpose or value. Increasingly I understood the negative effects of the domestic stereotype, as the only or best model, but was loath to discard it altogether for fear of losing my support system or my sense of identity as a woman.

## Realisation

It was not until the end of my ordination training that I began seriously to question my received world-view as regards gender. As a young mother immersed in babies, the feminist furore of the early seventies had largely passed me by. (I had married as soon as my Fine Art Diploma was completed, and become pregnant almost immediately, in retreat from the complexities of adult life.) I knew only the media caricatures of 'man-hating bra burners', and dismissed what I saw as extreme, hysterical and most definitely 'non-Christian'.

Later, with a husband in training for ordination and our sons well beyond infancy, I began to realise that the possibilities of a life outside the home had become attractive, that I too wanted the opportunity to have my vocation to public ministry tested. I was not then, in 1979, prepared to commit myself in the debate about women priests; words like 'strident' and 'pushy' frightened me, challenging my still fragile feminine identity as well as my perception of women as 'supporters' rather than leaders. I saw myself as 'privileged to serve' and the deaconess role, then the accredited ministry open to women, as quite sufficient. It was not until the final term of training, alongside and identical to the male ordinands', when discussing the essential nature of priesthood, that I awoke. 'But they have trained us to be *priests!*' The realisation brought an immediate sense of exclusion.

Once in ministry, as my confidence grew, so did my pain and my anger. Looking for a 'positive' way of dealing with these uncomfortable feelings, I attempted to rationalise and suppress them, thinking of my situation as some sort of identification with the marginalised and the rejection Christ had suffered. Then, at a conference, I attended a workshop on 'Women's issues in the Church'. The speaker recounted her experience of choosing to sing '*She who would valiant be*' at her daughter's baptism, and discovering that she could not sing for tears. It was a revelation to me. Our school hymn, sung with enthusiasm by 800 girls and 100 female staff had been the normal 'He' version and it had never crossed my mind as incongruous. It seemed that all the inconsistencies that I had tried to hold together were suddenly exposed, and I was at last forced to acknowledge them and to become fully aware of my feelings. Clare Herbert comments: 'There is evidence that women, schooled in our society to please others in looks, dress and behaviour from an early age so that they successfully "fit" in with life in a male-dominated world as they mature may have particular difficulty in expressing negative emotion.'[2] I would add, not only expressing, but recognising that they exist. As I did so I understood that not only my mother, but my school and church had given the same mixed messages: to be a 'real' disciple had meant being like Peter or James or John; the closest a woman could get was to dress up like Joan of Arc, or resign herself to the properly feminine role of penitent sinner, of Mary choosing the good part, or the 'sweet catholic girl' image I then had of the Virgin

Mary. No wonder that to follow some sort of vocation to a public role in the church was so confusing and painful.

I had been trying to believe all the conflicting messages at once; now I had to choose. I began to notice the sexist language used in church, at first reluctantly. For years I had proclaimed loudly that I knew I was included when the term 'men' was used to describe human beings. I came to see that to acknowledge my exclusion was painful, to meet indifference or hostility when the subject was discussed, more so. Coming to some sort of resolution of that conflict has been my journey of the last several years. To some extent I shall continue to struggle with my sense of my own femininity, as well as how far it is helpful or possible to move the theological goal posts. But I was prepared at last, rather late in the day, to look at the issues honestly, to try to reflect on my experience rather than accept the received wisdom, to call myself 'a feminist'.

## *What sort of feminist?*

This change in my perceptions has gradually come to mean a hope for a changed world; for a new awareness for both men and women of who they each are as individuals; for the affirmation of women, as well as men, as made in the image of God, reflecting the person and nature of God, to be received and honoured by all. It has brought, in large measure, an end to the war within me, to the negation of my body, the fear and rejection of my personality and the despising of weakness and vulnerability as 'womanish'. Feminism, which once seemed incompatible with Christianity, now seems intrinsically bound up with the gospel of Christ, as a message of freedom and the righting of wrongs, not just for women but also for men. I have come to acknowledge something of the oppression of men, encouraged from an early age to take on responsibility, to be required to solve problems and suppress all feelings of weakness or hurt. As I reflected on my reaction to the *Casablanca* excerpt, it occurred to me how the injunction to a little boy to 'look after Mummy, while I am gone', might suggest defending the home from burglars or attack, while the same words directed to a girl, would normally mean doing chores or bringing a cup of tea. Men too suffer in a patriarchal society, and the perpetrators and teachers of these values are generally women, who have not been able to recognise or name their own oppression or self-contempt. Understood in this way, feminism means a commitment to recognise and honour the sacredness of every individual, to seek wholeness for all people, working for changes in ourselves and in society, to live as stewards of creation, labouring with God to create 'the beloved community'.

This broadening of my understanding of feminism from the personal to the global grew initially out of struggling in an Equal Opportunities Working Party in the Diocese. Representatives from various 'minority' groups (disabled, black and gay) as well as women, all actively involved in our own struggle, but not necessarily aware of each other's worlds, spent several months trying to establish how we could work together. We discovered, through listening to each other, that we shared the same experience of being unheard and unseen, and a sense that our stories were valuable and needed to be heard, not only in order to induce change, but as reflections of the suffering of the world, the suffering of Christ. Some feminists would claim that all oppression, all evil, is rooted in patriarchy:

> The power men everywhere wield over women, power which has become a model for every other form of exploitation and illegitimate control ... would go as far as to say that before slavery or class

domination existed, men built an approach to women that would serve one day to introduce differences among us all.³

This seems to imply a fundamental blame attaching to the male sex, as unrealistic and offensive as that in the past attributed to Eve and through her to all women, as well as a *naïveté* about human nature. But it is undoubtedly true that the effect of all kinds of oppression bears a similar character, as witnessed by the experience of African American women: 'We often find it difficult to separate race from class and sex oppression because in our lives they are most often experienced simultaneously.'⁴

Many of us dream of how it might be in a church where each individual is valued and affirmed, encouraged and enabled to exercise and offer their unique gifts, for the good of all, where men would be set free to weep as women are to lead, where God's nurturing care will be as real to us as his power and authority, 'where the wolf shall live with the lamb ... and a little child shall lead them'. It is a powerful vision, one that inspires and excites and rightly so. Is it realistic? And if so, how do we move towards it? What do women priests bring? What if any are the pitfalls? What is the cost and what the hope for the future?

If we accept that human beings are weak and sinful, and that their full redemption is yet to come, that dream cannot be completely realisable in this life. Nor is the empowering or ordination of women the panacea for the ills of the church and the world. But the experience that women are now bringing to leadership roles, as well as the experience of having women as priests, *is* of immense significance. If we can keep a sense of perspective, if we will listen to each other, if we will be committed to continuing to learn and grow, we can and will move towards the realisation of the dream, which is the kingdom.

## What do women priests bring?

The symbolic significance of women priests being seen at the altar cannot be overestimated. Hard as it is to define exactly what it means or conveys, I am convinced that at a deep level something is being changed, and I suspect it is our picture of God. Sandra Schneiders, commenting on the situation for Roman Catholic women, refers to their 'sense of sacral unworthiness' and 'total sacramental dependence on men'. 'Women's exclusion from orders reinforces their subordination in all spheres because it divinizes maleness and conversely excludes femaleness from the sphere of the divine.' Inevitably the absence of women visibly acting as channels of God's grace and power 'has limited, distorted and subverted the Christian identity of women'.[5] Some have reacted to their first experiences of seeing a woman celebrate with 'It was wonderful, it wasn't different at all', others that they were profoundly aware of a difference, usually using words like 'completeness' and 'wholeness'. Whatever the conscious response, I believe the effect is deeply significant.

Some feminist theologians argue for the need to image God as Goddess, and Great Mother, Christ as 'Christa', in order to counterbalance aeons of patriarchy and affirm women's power and the goodness of their bodies. But to move so far beyond the received tradition of the church moves beyond Christianity as we have understood the term. Yet, within the church, women priests cannot but suggest, at some level, the neglected biblical images of God as mother and midwife, as well as the largely hidden strands of Christian spirituality that have always emphasised the nurturing aspects of God, and God's tenderness and intimacy. Yet this highlights the difficulty, that we may once more seem to be saying that men are representative of one particular aspect of God's nature and women another. As we become more accustomed to women taking a symbolic sacramental role, we may be clearer about the distinction between 'the feminine and the masculine' as opposed to the specific qualities of individual men and women. Perhaps then we can move towards a vision of who we are, together and individually, made in the image of God the Trinity: creator, lover, mother, friend, protector, sacrifice, redeemer, father, holy wisdom, mighty wind, vulnerable one, whispered word and blazing fire of love.

Apart from the symbolic impact of women priests, women's relational skills and experience promise much to bring about a relaxing and declericalising within the church: 'We can expect ever more emphasis on mutuality, shared responsibility, nonauthoritarian policies and procedures, and basic humaneness in operation as concern for persons catches up with our overly developed concern for institutions.'[6] Because of both their life experience and also the models with which they grew up, women are often adept at gathering people together, creating community and getting alongside others. Jean Baker Miller comments of adolescent development:

> The girl's sense of self esteem is based on feeling that she is part of relationships and is taking care of those relationships. This is very different from the components of self esteem as usually described and, incidentally, as measured by most available scales.
>
> ... the girl is seeking fulfilment ... within a context that will fulfill her great desire to be a 'being-in-relationship' ... The boy ... has the same needs, at bottom. However, he has been much more preoccupied with trying to develop 'himself' and a sense

of his independent identity. The culture has made the very heavy demand that he be so preoccupied. . .

Thus girls are not seeking the *kind* of identity that has been prescribed for boys, but a different kind, one in which one is a 'being-in-relationship', which means developing all of one's self in increasingly complex ways, in increasingly complex relationships.[7]

Within the church, ordained women have often spent years in assistant posts and been used to working with colleagues and sometimes in ways and worship styles that are not of their choice. They are used to team-building and supporting others, and have much to share with their male colleagues. There is an opportunity here for a real turning round from negative to positive. While feminism rightly warns us against clinging to a 'victim' role, so often appropriated by the oppressed in a way that paralyses and colludes with the situation, the experience of the women who have struggled together is a gift the church needs. There is a challenge to rediscover the tradition of God as liberator, to remind ourselves of the ideal of early Israel, a community of freed slaves who had no need of a king, and of Jesus who called his followers 'friends'.

I referred earlier to the wisdom communicated in 'traditional' women's groups. In part these referred to parenting and home-making skills, as well as agreeing how to 'manage' men, for an inevitable, if regrettable corollary of accepting restriction of one's powers is a tendency towards manipulative behaviour. This 'women's wisdom' was also to a great extent concerned with the development of a multi-skilled approach to life, generally denigrated in the professional world. I used to dread having to declare myself 'just a housewife', but the responsibility for managing a household of people of various ages is no simple matter. A wide variety of skills are necessary, usually exercised several at a time. The list might include child carer, nursery nurse, driver, gardener, social and business secretary, accountant, teacher, medical nurse, cook, cleaner, painter/decorator, organiser, voluntary worker, confidante and counsellor – nothing if not stretching. Added to that the situation for many women clergy of working, or having worked, part time or in split jobs, non-stipendiary or in a parish other than where they live, means that they are unusually well equipped for the changing nature of the church today, with its growing emphasis on adaptability.

The numbers of women exploring the possibility of ordained ministry are increasing, as are those considering lay ministry of various sorts. It seems that the arrival of women priests has provided immediate 'role models', envisioning and releasing many women. As women priests grow in confidence, they will increasingly feel free to use female biblical models, and use them in a more positive way. I commented, above, on my realisation that 'the disciples' had always been presented to me as the twelve apostles, and that women were almost exclusively given as examples of neediness. Alongside the apostles and saints, I now want to give emphasis to stories such as that of the Canaanite woman, who insisted and argued her case for a healing (Matthew 15.21ff); of Mary's proclamation of Jesus as the Christ, alongside Peter's (John 11.27); of the woman who anointed Jesus' head in priestly style (Mark 14.3ff); of the faithful disciples at the cross (Mark 15.40ff); and of Mary Magdalene, first witness to the resurrection (John 20.11), as well as those of the great women of faith: Miriam, Deborah, Hannah, Ruth and Esther and our mothers, Eve, Sarah, Rachel and Rebecca so often excluded from the lists.

Spiritual direction is still largely the preserve of men, in that most directors are clergymen, and they have written most of the books on prayer. Yet, it is women who have long been recognised in the West as 'the pray-ers'. Social factors account for this in part, where women at home may be more able to arrange times of privacy, as does the emphasis on the more 'feminine' attributes of openness, intuition, waiting, silence and passivity. It is also significant that private prayer has been the one religious activity in which women could engage without a male intermediary. Feminist approaches to spiritual direction for women have moved away from traditional models, stressing 'a focus on women's experience as the authoritative starting point for spirituality; the importance of recognising the social as well as personal roots of women's spiritual issues; the need to demystify the power relationship inherent in any helping process.'[8] As this field develops and as women increasingly take on the role of spiritual direction, working in new ways with both men and women, it will be interesting to discover whether lay men begin to find a vocation to pray, alongside the women and male clergy.

## The pitfalls

Human beings have a tendency towards dualism at all sorts of levels, projecting our bad and uncomfortable feelings out onto individuals or groups different from our own. It is tidy and enables us to simplify the issues and, by so doing, to avoid facing ourselves. My difficulty with the more extreme expressions of feminism is just this lack of realism that envisages a whole new creation springing from an end to patriarchy. It has to be more complex and more mysterious, if we proclaim a God who is committed to working within a fallen world and who is revealed both as self-giving love, and as the transcendent power of absolute authority. Audre Lorde, a black feminist, writes:

> We have all been programmed to respond to the

human differences between us with fear and loathing and to handle that difference in one of three ways: ignore it, and if that is not possible, copy it if we think it is dominant, or destroy it if we think it is subordinate.[9]

But despite our programming, our backgrounds, fears, prejudices and limitations, we can and do venture beyond the terrible cycle of repeated oppression. While I am conscious of my status as among the most privileged: white, middle-class, professional and heterosexual, I want to assert that there is hope for the human situation and of establishing new ways of relating to each other. Not all of us will move on from our learned behaviour, and we may not progress very far or fast, but some are able to change the pattern and they beckon us forwards. As we begin to recognise our distrust and fear of ourselves and others, we are enabled to change, in Christian terms to begin to be made whole. As we have the responsibility for bringing others with us, we have to accept that the pace will be slow, and to remember that the redemption of the world does not rest with human beings alone!

*The cost and the hope*

Most of us dread change above all else and the move, the holiday, the new job, the divorce, sickness, retirement and bereavement score highest on the stress questionnaires. Change is hard because it requires us to change, and that means work and loss – and yet we pray 'your kingdom come', at least with our lips. So the coming of the kingdom, of the small part of the kingdom that we are struggling to bring to birth, is costly for us, and the change required must be accomplished as much in ourselves as in others. Counsellors tell us that in any situation a person has three choices: to leave, to accept, or to change.

Many women are tempted to despair at the slow rate of advance for women, both within the church and beyond it; there is a constant sense of 'one step forwards, two steps back', and often a sense of betrayal at the intransigence of other women. The *Casablanca* romantic myth has something to do with this, and it is interesting to note that research shows that it is older women in the church who are most offended by sexist language. It is as if having accepted the *status quo* all their lives, they have come to see that after all they are not included. Audre Lorde again:

> It is easy for white women to believe the dangerous fantasy that if you are good enough, pretty enough, sweet enough, quiet enough, teach the children to behave, hate the right people, and marry the right men, then you will be allowed to co-exist with patriarchy in relative peace, at least until a man needs your job or your neighbourhood rapist happens along.[10]

But we are not to despair: in any situation the most effective change that we can realise is the change in ourselves, and we all still have much work to do. 'Women's choices are frequently skewed by timidity and fear in the face of autonomous action, self-hatred born of internalised oppression and an anxiety that leads to evasion and helplessness.'[11] Women are becoming increasingly self aware and coming to recognise their need to change. Indeed the priesting of women forced many to face the fact that being the victim had become something of a habit, and that to 'take authority', as bidden in the ordinal, meant engaging in personal work and shifting one's own perceptions. Both lay and ordained women together are signing up for all sorts of assertiveness courses, and discovering in Womenchurch and Womenfaith groups the possibility of exploring and interpreting their experiences as women, engaging with the gospel. We are moving, and it is often hard work, particularly in areas where there is ambivalence:

> Women do fear admitting that they want or need power ... the big fear [is] of being seen as wanting to be powerful, this provoke[s] notions of disapproval ... [and] at a deeper level ... fears of attack and ultimate abandonment by all women and men ... [F]or many women it is more comfortable to feel inadequate ... than to feel powerful, if power makes you feel destructive.[12]

If we are to have power over our lives, in other words if we are to become fully adult, we first have to acknowledge our conflicting feelings, and what we have to gain as well as to lose. Certainly traditionally women have been most at ease acknowledging their use of power on behalf of others, just as they are often only able openly to express anger in defence of others. 'Concepts such as "fear of owning one's power", "identification with the victim", "fear of success", and the "Cinderella syndrome" describe women as they deviate from the more traditional models of power and action.'[13] It is an ongoing struggle, but if women are prepared to work with each other and find the confidence to offer what they learn, I believe they have the potential to bring a renewed vision to the church:

> Out of this, we can see that women already may have a strong motivation to approach the concept of power with a different, critical, and creative stance. Once admitting a desire and need for power, women can seek new ways of negotiating power with others in personal life, work, and other institutions ... the fact that it sounds unreal must not stop us.[14]

And *Casablanca*? To some extent the myth holds, the dance between the sexes depends on taking different steps, playing different roles. My hope is that we can continue to enjoy the 'dance', while acknowledging that it is only part of the story and that the roles can also interchange and overlap. As women continue to learn that they are capable not only of achieving all that men have achieved, but of making those roles their own, of doing it differently, as well as doing it 'the same'; men will increasingly recover their confidence, where they have been threatened, and be freed to learn as well as to teach, to receive as well as to give. That is the dream, that together we shall create ever new and more complex patterns of relating, freeing rather than confining each other, and reflecting and releasing the infinite energy, variety and richness of God.

## Notes

1 Jean Baker Miller, 'The development of women's sense of self' in *Women's Growth in Connection: Writings from the Stone Center* (The Guilford Press, 1991), p. 11.
2 Clare Herbert, 'A resounding silence' in Sue Walrond-Skinner (ed.), *Crossing the Boundary: What Will Women Priests Mean?* (Mowbray, 1994), p. 41.
3 Adrienne Rich, *Blood, Bread and Poverty: Notes Towards a Politics of Location* (New York: W. W. Norton, 1984), p. 217.
4 1977 Combahee River Collective Statement, quoted in Rich, *Blood, Bread and Poverty*, p. 218.
5 Sandra M. Schneiders, 'The effect of women's experience on their spirituality' in Joann Wolski Conn (ed.), *Women's Spirituality: Resources for Christian Development* (New York: Paulist Press, 1986), pp. 33–4.
6 Schneiders, 'Women's experience', p. 37.
7 Miller, 'Women's sense of self', pp. 16 and 21.
8 Kathleen Fischer, *Women at the Well: Feminist Perspectives on Spiritual Direction* (New York: Paulist Press, 1988), p. 6.

9 Audre Lorde, *Sister Outsider* (New York: The Crossing Press, 1984), pp. 115–19.
10 ibid.
11 Jean Baker Miller, 'Women and power' in *Women's Growth in Connection*, pp. 200–2.
12 Miller, 'Women and power', pp. 200ff.
13 Janet L. Surrey, 'Relationship and empowerment' in *Women's Growth in Connection*, p. 166.
14 Miller, 'Women and power', p. 205.

# 7 From expectations to realities:

## And the future

PATIENCE PURCHAS

On 21 January 1984 a thousand people filled the nave of Westminster Abbey for a service to celebrate the fortieth anniversary of the first ordination of a woman to the priesthood in the Anglican Communion. Florence Li Tim Oi, who had been ordained by Bishop R. O. Hall of Hong Kong and South China in the difficult years of the Japanese occupation of much of China, had become an inspiration to many of those engaged in the Movement for the Ordination of Women. Her presence at the Abbey was a sign of hope, particularly to the large number of deaconesses who travelled to London for the service. The *Church Times* reported: 'There was a long blue stream of deaconesses, at once an impressive and a poignant sight, impressive because of the smartness and dignity of bearing of the women; poignant because, almost certainly, many of them in that procession feel a calling to the priesthood.'

As the procession of deaconesses moved into the Abbey they were met by the already assembled male priests who were smiling in welcome and standing with an empty chair beside each man. The deaconesses moved forward to fill the spaces, giving a powerful visual image of what a whole priesthood, shared by men and women, could look like. It seemed a vision of something more than

© 1996 Patience Purchas

equality, that here God was transforming priesthood into something new and good.

That vision was needed to sustain those who longed to see women priests in the Church of England. There were testing times in the years leading up to the final vote in General Synod on 11 November 1992. The long process of education and persuasion had its peaks and troughs, as has been well documented, but it became clear that a large majority in the church were ready to accept women priests. There were wild threats of vast numbers of priests and laypeople preparing to leave the Church of England if women were ordained priest, but probably most believed that what was called the 'conscience provision' would suffice to hold the church together. Expectations and emotions were high on both sides when the great debate finally took place in General Synod. In the event, the arguments were presented with clarity, conviction and, on the whole, courteous restraint. The vote in favour of women priests was greeted in silence, as is the custom in General Synod. The inevitable rejoicing outside Church House, Westminster was furiously condemned by some. While people in parishes up and down the land, and many people who claimed no Anglican or even Christian allegiance, were expressing delight that at last this Rubicon had been crossed, the church at the centre appeared to go into mourning.

The bishops, it seems, set their unity above everything else and worked to find a way of holding that unity in view of the fact that a number of them had voted against the legislation. It was reported that they sang hymns of thanksgiving when they found a way of achieving unity at a meeting in Manchester. The need to get Parliamentary approval through the Ecclesiastical Committee, which was weighted heavily against women priests, required some tight negotiating. Codes of practice and, finally, the Act of Synod fleshed out the conscience provision made in the 1992 legislation. The outcome was that no diocese became a 'no-go' area for women priests but considerable concessions were made. The most significant of these was the introduction of a concept of provisionality in the reform. This is usually referred to in terms of the Gamaliel principle ('If this plan or this undertaking is of human origin, it will fail; but if it is of God, you will not be able to overthrow them – in that case you might even be found fighting against God!' Acts 5.38–9 (NRSV) ). Previously the talk had been of reception, of allowing a decent period of time for people to get used to the new thing and either find a way of living with it or leave with suitable compensation if that proved impossible. Few can seriously imagine the legislation admitting women to the priesthood will ever be rescinded, but a new element of uncertainty about the decision was introduced. The introduction of the concept of provisionality was defended by the Archbishop of York during the debate in General Synod on the Act of Synod.

> ... the shift from reception to discernment ... yes indeed, that is deliberate. We are trying to think of this within the context of the Church universal and 'reception' implied to some that we had to move inevitably in one direction. We believe we are moving in that direction, but we have also to be sufficiently open to listening to what our fellow Christians in other traditions are saying. That is why the word 'discernment' is in.

Not much comfort there for those who thought the Church of England, after many years' discussion, had made its mind up.

Following the meeting of the House of Bishops in Manchester another significant expression emerged with talk of two integrities in the church. The expression has been widely taken up, despite attempts to drop it. What began as a decision made by a large majority for the whole of the Church of England has come to be seen as one of two equally valid understandings. Thus it is now acceptable to hold the view that there are two kinds of priesthood in the Church of England. Most people recognise that both men and women who have been canonically ordained are truly priests in the church of God. A minority may respectably hold the view that women so ordained are not priests at all and the sacraments they administer are invalid. As the months have passed the two integrities become ever more firmly established. There is a constant pressure from those opposed to the priesthood of women for further concessions. While some have been resisted, others have been accepted, notably in the area of episcopal appointments. There are now three Provincial Episcopal Visitors, the so-called 'flying bishops', who care for the interests of those opposed to women priests. The appointments of new bishops opposed to women priests and the recent appointment of the Bishop of London (who is a leading opponent of the priesthood of women) as Archbishop of York establishes the position of those who will not recognise the validity of the orders of women priests for some time to come.

Opinions are divided as to whether the provision made for opponents of women priests is appropriate, though the Act of Synod received large majorities in support in General Synod. Some opponents are grateful for concessions which have allowed them to remain in the church. Others ask for much more and speak in terms of persecution. Indeed, the level of bitterness and distress shown has led some who voted for the legislation to say they would not have done so had they known what it would be like. Many proponents believe that generosity and inclusiveness are hallmarks of the Christian faith and that the arrangements are a reasonable price to pay. Others are unhappy about the implications of the conscience provision for the church as a whole and the ministry of women priests in particular. Some laypeople particularly resent the whole package and point out that no other organisation would be so generous to those who disagree with a policy decision. Time will tell which viewpoint is valid. What is clear is that the situation is complicated and sometimes uncomfortable for all sides. Women and men who had hoped that the positive vote in 1992 would open the way to the kind of reformed and liberated priesthood envisaged in the Westminster Abbey service have had to come to terms with constraints and frustrations that many had probably not anticipated. The Bishop of Ely, speaking in General Synod when the Act of Synod was debated in November 1993, offered words of support and encouragement.

> As women in holy orders . . . they will experience the pain of the fact that this ministry is not recognised by all Christians . . . No-one, conscious of the long and baleful history of the oppression of women, can fail to realise what it will mean for them in terms of their own confidence in God's promises, his call and their costly obedience . . . But let there be no doubt, in ordaining women the Church will be acting as Christ's Holy Catholic and Apostolic Church . . . The orders the women priests will receive will be orders in the Church of God.

The first ordination of women as priests in the Church of England took place in Bristol Diocese in March 1994. For a while the mood seemed to change in the church. At long last the bishops felt able to express pleasure at the outcome of the November 1992 vote. The affirmation of their ministry the women had waited for was heard. Cathedrals were filled with joyful congregations and the church seemed to be looking forward with hope. At the end of 1994 there were 1,340 ordained women in the church and 10,808 ordained men. These figures include deacons as well as priests but almost all the deacons would go on to become priests within a year. Women now represent 12.4% of the clergy. Their deployment throughout the Church of England is, however, very uneven. There were, for instance, 5 stipendiary (paid) women clergy in Truro Diocese at the end of 1994 and 123 stipendiary men (4.7% women). At the same time in Bristol Diocese there were 25 stipendiary women and 148 men (16.9% women). To some extent the figures represent the tradition within each diocese and the views of the diocesan bishop on the ordination of women. Some dioceses, where the bishop has taken a strong line against the ordination of women, have attracted large numbers of like-minded priests, and women priests are less welcome. Nonetheless, there are now women priests in every diocese of the Church of England, though Sodor and Man has only one!

A further significant distinction between the deployment of men and women is that whereas nationally only 10.5% of ordained men are non-stipendiary (unpaid), 41.5% of the women are non-stipendiary. Non-stipendiary ministry is a fairly new phenomenon in the Church of England and regarded with suspicion by some. It developed as a response to the need for more clergy than the church could afford to employ and also out of recognition that there are men and women able and willing to give some of their spare time to ministry in a voluntary capacity. Non-stipendiaries are selected according to the same criteria as stipendiaries but normally trained locally. The amount of time they give to ministry varies from a few hours on Sundays to full time. Many dioceses will only use non-stipendiaries as assistants but some dioceses are willing to place them in charge of a parish, particularly if they are willing to move and live there. The status of non-stipendiaries varies from diocese to diocese. In some they are treated on an equal footing with their paid counterparts, in others they are more like second-class citizens, denied access to clergy chapter meetings, for instance.

There are various reasons for the imbalance in the proportion of women who are non-stipendiary. It is a curious characteristic of the way women's ministry has been allowed to develop and must be untypical of other professions. It is hard to imagine, for instance, women solicitors, accountants or doctors accepting a situation where nearly half their profession were expected to work unpaid because they were women. In part the situation arose in the church because women were not able to be ordained and so could not minister the sacraments. The ministry open to them was essentially pastoral and this was seen as appropriate to assistant rather than leadership posts.

The imbalance is often accounted for by the difficulty of deploying married women outside their home parishes, particularly those with children. A significant minority of ordained women are married to priests who are normally required to live within their parish. Some dioceses are unwilling to pay both partners of an ordained couple on the principle that a clergy stipend is not a salary but the provision of enough money to enable a clergy family to live independently. Traditionally, clergy wives have given unstintingly of their time in a supportive ministry to their husbands and there is an anxiety about appearing to devalue this if other women, even though they have been selected, trained and ordained, are paid to minister. In any case there is still a strongly held view in some dioceses that a woman's place is that of the supportive wife at home looking after her family and there is concern that the church should not be seen to be undermining family life. Some take the view that where paid jobs are getting more scarce, the jobs should go to men rather than married women. All of which overlooks the fact that some of the women in ministry are single.

There are ways round all these problems and there are some outdated understandings around, but where there is resistance to change progress is slow. It is important to say in all this that many women non-stipendiaries are happy with their lot and see it as their vocation, thankful that they are able to offer ministry to the church without remuneration. It is also important to say that there are women who feel exploited by a church which uses their time, talents and gifts but expects to get them free. There certainly needs to be greater clarity in future in identifying those who are non-stipendiary by choice from those who would welcome a stipend were one forthcoming.

Many of the women who were ordained in 1994 had long experience of ministry. Some had served seven years in the diaconate with maybe years as a deaconess before that. (The diaconate was opened to women in 1987.) Because they were not priests none had been able to be incumbents of parishes as vicar or rector, though some had been given responsibility for the oversight of parishes. It was reasonable to expect that such experienced and able women would rapidly move into the posts of responsibility they would have held had they been men. Just as there is a wide variation in the numbers of women priests in dioceses so there has been in the development of their ministry. Portsmouth is a small diocese with a bishop who voted against the ordination of women. To the surprise of some and the disappointment of others he was willing to ordain women as priests once the decision had been taken. Of the seven women who held stipendiary posts at the end of 1994 two are incumbents, one is a residentiary canon and one holds a senior diocesan post. A priest in the diocese said that the ministry of women was given a high profile. In Coventry Diocese, where all the senior staff are in favour of the ordination of women and a large majority voted in favour at the Diocesan Synod, progress has been slower. Out of the total of forty women priests, three women are team vicars (a responsible though subordinate role), one woman is a residentiary canon, two hold diocesan posts and one woman will shortly be made an incumbent. A priest in Coventry Diocese felt that developing the ministry of women was not seen as a high priority. In the Diocese of St Albans, where again the diocesan senior staff are all in favour of the ordination of women, there are now seventy-three women priests, thirty-three of whom are stipendiary. Of these, five are now incumbents, one is priest in charge of a parish, two are team vicars and one is a member of the bishop's staff.

Some dioceses have no women as incumbents as yet. There is anecdotal evidence that some bishops are unwilling to enable the appointment of women as incumbents lest they wound the sensibilities of those priests in the diocese who are opposed to women priests. It is also said that some bishops will not license a woman to a parish while there are male priests seeking livings. One of the practical outcomes of holding women back in this way is that able women change diocese when they can, moving to greener pastures. The effect, if this trend continues, will be to accentuate the uneven development of women's ministry, with the green pastures becoming ever richer and the stony ground becoming a desert. The bishops might like to consider that there is more than one kind of no-go area.

The patchy development seems to relate to a number

of factors. The attitude of the bishop and his staff is clearly one. Without the bishop's support it is hard for women's priestly ministry to take off. A form of tokenism seems to happen in some dioceses where the bishop is unhappy about women priests. He will see that one or two women are given incumbencies and may encourage the appointment of a woman as a residentiary canon but, having made his token gesture, may leave it at that. Where bishops have wanted to be seen positively to encourage their ministry, women are moving into senior posts.

Another factor seems to be the groundwork done in previous years. Several years before the priesthood was open to women the Board of Ministry in St Albans Diocese backed a programme of persuasion and challenge, designed to identify posts of responsibility for women, called 'Your next vicar could be a woman'. Presentations took place at large meetings with guest speakers and at the Diocesan Synod. Every Deanery Pastoral Committee was visited and challenged to identify posts that might be held by women. At the time it aroused interest in some places, anxiety in others and a small amount of wrath, but bore the fruits of an openness to women's ministry which paved the way for greater things after 1994. If nothing else, it raised the profile of women's ministry and encouraged parishes to want to experience that ministry by at least inviting ordained women to preach. The fear of the unknown or novel was overcome and frequently the women had the experience of being told something like 'I thought I wouldn't like seeing a woman preaching/ leading worship/taking a funeral, but it was all right.' In dioceses like St Albans where there were a large number of women deacons an expectancy had grown up that looked forward to their ministry as priests.

The third factor seems to be the proportion of priests opposed to women's ministry. In some dioceses those opposed are a small minority, and that number made up of people who work courteously with the system and others who are vociferously obstructive. On the whole, the dioceses with many priests opposed to ordained women have bishops who share their view. It tends to follow that the welcome to women priests is considerably more generous in some dioceses than others.

A fourth factor is the attitude and expectation of the women priests themselves. It is a characteristic of some of the first generation of women priests that they have an anxiety about causing trouble, rocking the boat, being the focus of strife or being seen to ask for things for themselves. They have learnt to be compliant and submissive and grateful for very small mercies because in the past that was the only way their ministry was accepted. Where women feel unable to challenge the *status quo*, or think it inappropriate to ask for what they need, they are likely to remain as assistants for ever. The sad thing is that some in the church will congratulate them for their unassuming service and contribution to a quiet life.

More than a year after the first ordinations, the women priests are sometimes asked 'How has it been?' Inevitably there have been positive and negative experiences, and within any one diocese there are likely to be different experiences, though, as has already been indicated, the attitude in some dioceses as a whole is considerably more welcoming than in others. There is a certain frustration in some places that the pace of change has seemed so slow. The long hiatus between the vote and the ordinations was hard as was the enormous amount of attention given to those who were distressed by the result. The church is sometimes less than gracious when it relates to women in ministry. It was made clear in some places that the women must expect their interests to be subordinated to those of men in ministry. There were situations at the time of the first ordinations when women were expected to move from parishes because a few parishioners were registering their dissent. 'Magnanimity in victory' is the key phrase in one diocese I was told about, with the implication that nothing must be done that might cause distress. 'They have served so long and borne the burden in the heat of the day,' another bishop explained. The women who had served in the church's ministry for fifteen, twenty or thirty years might wonder what value that placed on their work.

There has been disappointment and anger that women have found difficulty in getting suitable work in some dioceses. There may well have been an unrealistic expectation about the speed of change in the church and, in a few cases, an over-estimate of people's abilities. It seems likely that a small number of the women ordained in 1994 would not have been ordained in any other circumstances, and they are now proving hard to employ. In the past, the church has found posts for some very strange male priests. (A senior clergyman once said: 'God in his infinite wisdom and generosity allows some men to be employed by the church who would, in any other circumstances, be totally unemployable.') There is no reason to expect that the experience of women in the church will be different from any other of the professions as they have opened up to women. Women being considered for incumbencies and senior posts will have, on average, to be brighter candidates than the men. Sometimes women will find they are offered the difficult and less prestigious jobs. The good news is that where they have the grace to take on sad and neglected parishes and love them into life a positive message goes out that the priestly ministry of women, far from being second best, can be a blessing and a refreshment to the church.

A mood of caution seems to have percolated through the church. It might be expressed in such terms as 'Don't rush things, don't force issues, don't take risks; if in doubt, better not, it won't hurt the women to wait'. Where a common mind cannot be reached it seems sometimes to be the minority viewpoint, however unrepresentative, which is honoured. As in any big organisation, the power of inertia is formidable. Until there is a real will to challenge and push, the gifts of women are going to be under-utilised. It is common to see advertisements for incumbencies which say the parish is in favour of women priests but wants a man this time. The acronym NTT (Not This Time) could be joined by the insidious MPANRFTY (My People Are Not Ready For This Yet). There is provision in the legislation to cover situations in team and group ministries where agreement cannot be reached, but the provision is extended very generously. A recent advertisement for six very small parishes being informally linked together for the first time made it clear that the desire of five parishes to have the option of considering women candidates was to be abandoned because one village would not welcome a woman priest. In another situation it is the objection of two families which is blocking the appointment of a woman to a parish. It is consonant with the current climate in the church that this was considered acceptable.

The church is no different from many organisations in being deeply patriarchal and sometimes misogynist. Although women outnumber men in the pews, the church is largely male-led and working to male norms. Even where women are sincerely welcome they find they are constantly having to remind their colleagues that things have changed. This might be as simple a matter as pointing out that 'brethren', the traditional greeting at a clerical gathering, will no longer do. At a meeting of the Diocesan Synod in my own diocese, discussing clergy conditions of service, it was necessary to remind speakers that it was no longer appropriate to use the word 'clergymen' as a group term for the ordained ministry and to remind people that some of the clergy have husbands rather than wives. Language significantly reflects people's mind-set and the church is being asked to change its terminology as it has changed its mind. Women will no doubt have to put up with protests and silly jokes about 'hymns and hers' for some time. There is a cost for both of the sexes, of course. I remember a significant moment when I spoke to the incumbents of the women who were to be ordained priest in my own diocese. I spoke of the ordained ministry as an all-male club which many of them enjoyed and which would never be the same again once women joined it. The room went very quiet as the men reflected that there would be loss for them in the reform they all welcomed so warmly. Some men have taken the attitude that since women wanted to join their club so they must learn the rules and play by them, and this can harden into a refusal to compromise or make allowances. 'If you can't stand the heat get out of the kitchen . . .' The women might well point out that they have plenty of kitchen experience and some new recipes to share.

Some dioceses have a post held by a woman who has responsibility for women's ministry. There is a wide range of job descriptions for such posts. At one end of the spectrum there are posts where the woman is a member of the bishop's staff, attending regular meetings and having responsibility for oversight and development of women's ministry. Her presence at that level will serve not just to keep issues of women's ministry to the fore and enable that ministry to develop but also to provide a feminine perspective on a whole range of issues, and be a constant reminder that the priesthood is no longer all male. In other dioceses such posts are restricted significantly by excluding the woman from the staff meetings unless there are issues seen as specifically relating to women on the agenda. In other places tokenism again prevails and a woman who may be quite junior is given a title but no power or authority. One or two dioceses have chosen to have women's interests represented by a man. This can be perverse, a way of putting women down, or a benign attempt to assert that since women and men are equal in the ministry either can represent the needs of the other. Women are insulted by the former attitude and might point out in relation to the second that they do not yet experience equality in the church. When the playing field is level there will be no need for such posts, but many find it pretty bumpy at present.

The difficulties some women have encountered have had their toll. There is a tendency to speak of women priests directly or indirectly as a problem for the church. No one is supposed to talk about tainted hands, but the reality is that in some places the presence of a woman priest is seen as defiling. When people turn their heads away at the altar rail and refuse communion from a woman's hands, when a woman priest is asked not to robe and join other clergy in the sanctuary at a deanery service because her presence would cause offence, when a diocesan bishop will not lay his hands on the head of a woman to ordain her, when a man will not accept ordination at the hands of a bishop who has ordained women, there is a price to be paid. Many male priests will rightly say that they share in the cost, but it is the women who carry the weight of guilt and anxiety. It is no help to assure women that no offence is meant and no personal reflection intended. Nothing could be more personal than ordination to the priesthood. Indeed it is about the very being of the person. Women are sometimes made to feel guilty because they are causing such distress in the church, their very presence making some men renounce their orders and leave the Church of England. Women have to work out whether the guilt they feel is appropriate. Christians are called to take up a cross and follow Christ – they are not asked to take up guilt which they do not own. Christians are called to be caring, generous, forbearing and sacrificial but not to be unfaithful to their vocation.

For the last three years the Church of England has been going through a process of reformation. It has been an uncomfortable time of transition, rather like rearranging the furniture in a well-loved room. The decision to go for change was exhilarating and the hope that the room might take on a whole new look sustained the effort. But there comes a time in furniture-moving when the pieces get all mixed up, some in the new places and looking good, some stuck in the middle of the room, and you begin to wonder if it will ever fit together again. There may even be a temptation to wish you had never started and there will certainly be people who will tell you they preferred things the way they were. At these times it is good to take stock of what has been achieved and note the positive results. The truth is that there are many hopeful indicators. Women priests are well established as part of the ministry of the Church of England. Their ministry is being warmly received and welcomed in the parishes they serve. After the initial euphoria which marked the first celebrations of Holy Communion, people are taking their presence for granted, though there are still times when people will comment that they have never before seen a woman presiding or taking a wedding. The hurtful bitterness of a few negative reactions is wonderfully offset by the affirming remarks made by those who rejoice to see a woman priest. In chapters, synods and clergy conferences their presence is taken for granted. At ordination services, the presentation of women candidates is now expected and people get no more excited about their presence than about the male candidates. The long experience of women in the diaconate has meant that both parishes and the women themselves have the confidence to accept women priests in leadership roles. Women are growing in strength and learning to ask for what they need. Senior posts are beginning to open up, if slowly, and the ability of some of the most able women is being recognised. It is good that the Church of England will soon have its first woman Archdeacon, Canon Judith Rose.

There is still, of course, some distance to travel before men and women share in that transformed priesthood envisaged at Westminster Abbey in 1984. The work of education and persuasion which, under God, brought about the vote will need to continue. There is a fear of women becoming clericalised in a way that destroys their freedom, or of their adopting male norms uncritically. One of the best things to come out of the long struggle towards priesthood was the way lay and ordained women and men worked together for a common cause. That sharing must not be lost by women priests disappearing behind a spiritual icon screen. The sense of liberation and joy which many laywomen continue to feel when they see a woman at the altar has been one of the most important blessings derived from the ordination of women. Further, in a society where relations between men and women so often seem fractured or unhealthy the church has a chance to model a better way of relating. A recent in-service training conference looked at men and women working together in ministry. At the conclusion of the conference, the participants reflected on how significantly different it had felt to work with exactly equal numbers of men and women. There was no need to be competitive, nor to bolster a minority; instead the participants helped, supported and listened to each other and enjoyed a small foretaste of what the ministry could be like when more women were ordained.

Equal opportunities policies are standard in most places where women and men work together. The church is slowly waking up to the significantly changed situation since the decision to ordain women. It might well consider the evidence of a recent survey of the experience of women priests in New Zealand. That showed that sexual harassment was a problem for women in ministry. There are important issues here for the church to consider at local and national level. The church is at present engaged in an examination of the conditions of service of clergy but the discussion document takes almost no note of the particular needs of women. Maternity and paternity leave, arrangements for returning to work after a period of time devoted to child care, the possible payment for child care have hardly been considered. There is plenty of work yet to be done.

As women grow in confidence and experience it will become clear that there is one more river to cross. While there continues to be an all-male episcopate women will be disadvantaged. However benign, however sensitive the bishops may be, the total absence of women from their company when they make policy decisions already seems odd and will come to seem outrageous. Perhaps the oddest thing about it is that so few of the bishops seem to see anything wrong with the situation. It will be when there are women in the House of Bishops that a true partnership of men and women working together in ministry to the glory of God will be known. Until then, there is a great deal to be thankful for, some things to forgive and much to work for. It is time we put the traumas of the past behind, stopped looking over our shoulders and recognised that God has sent the priestly ministry of women as a blessing to the church. At many of the great ordination services in 1994 Timothy Dudley-Smith's hymn 'Lord of the years' was sung. It seemed to say what was needed of past hurt and future confidence:

> *Lord, for ourselves;*
>   *in living power remake us –*
> *self on the cross*
>   *and Christ upon the throne,*
> *past put behind us,*
>   *for the future take us,*
> *Lord of our lives,*
>   *to live for Christ alone.*

# 8 What difference is women's priesthood making to the Church of England?
JUDITH ROSE

The Church of England is just one expression of the church of God. It has its strengths and weaknesses but if it is in reality part of God's church then it is not just an institution or organisation – it is a living organism, inspired and sustained by the Spirit of the living God. Lively language is used in the New Testament to describe the church. It is, 'the vine with its branches',[1] and, 'the body of Christ'.[2] Living organisms, by definition, change. No change signifies death. The Church of England therefore, along with other expressions of the church of God, is always changing. That is in itself a healthy sign although there is always the judgement to be made about whether any particular change is for good or ill. The ordination of women to the priesthood within the Church of England, along with other factors, has already and inevitably meant change. How significant these changes prove to be and the difference it will make to the Church of England only time will tell. This book attempts to look at the potential for change brought about by this development and to anticipate what further changes there may be in its ministry and mission. The Church of England has survived and been enriched by significant changes over the centuries. We wait to see in what measure the ordination of women to the priesthood will bring a further enrichment.

© 1996 Judith Rose

In 1994 about 1,250 women were ordained to the priesthood within the Church of England. This did not of course represent 1,250 additional ministers. All of these women had been serving for at least a year within the diaconate and many of them had been serving in the church for a very long time before being permitted to test their vocation to the priesthood. We have women who are now priests who began their stipendiary ministry in the 1950s and 1960s as parish workers, later to become deaconesses and, when church law changed in 1987, to be made deacons. Many had carried significant responsibility in parochial work or sector ministry without the privilege of being ordained priest. In 1994 not only did the Church of England experience the new phenomenon of having women within the priesthood but many of these women brought to their priesthood a wealth of experience of ministry. This book has been researched and written within two years of these first ordinations. This is a short time in the life of any organisation and especially in the church of God. We are in an interesting and an emerging situation but it is too early to be dogmatic about the differences that this will make to the Church of England. Below are some indications of the way that things may be going. Only time will tell if I am right and to what extent.

The ordination of women to the priesthood has coincided with other changes facing the Church of England, not least the results of the financial situation brought about by changes in the fortunes of the Church Commissioners. This in turn is leading to changes in how the Church of England finances its work, to constraints on the number of clergy employed, in some places to a reduction in sector ministers and a reconsideration of the role of honorary and locally ordained clergy. The conditions under which clergy are deployed is also under review and could result in changes which demand better management structures, personnel services and levels of accountability and perhaps a further erosion of the freehold. There is a continuing development of lay ministries, which has been taking place over the last twenty years. This in turn means changing patterns of leadership in a parish with the clergy often part of a leadership team. The context in which the church serves is also changing. British society is becoming increasingly secular. No longer can it be assumed that the majority of the population have any Christian background. The English Church Census of 1989 revealed that only 14% of children under fifteen years of age are in a church-related activity on a typical Sunday. Added to this is a greater awareness of British citizens who have an allegiance to another faith. Alongside these issues are those that specifically affect women, such as the increase in the number of professional women in our society, and the growth of the feminist movement and of feminist theology.

With so much change happening at the same time as women are included in the priesthood of the Church of England it is not easy to isolate the changes that are directly associated with this particular development. However the following are probably significant.

### *Changing patterns of priesthood*

For the past twenty years or so there has been a high-profile, ongoing debate about whether women should or could be ordained to holy orders. This inevitably had an effect upon the women who were exercising a ministry in the Church of England as parish workers or deaconesses. Their own vocation was challenged and was under public scrutiny. Many of these women, myself included, felt and said that they were not ashamed to be women and that God had not made a mistake in this respect, but that they were also genuinely seeking to obey God's call to serve him within the formal ministry of the church. For many their call appeared to be similar to that of the men whose vocation found its fulfilment in priesthood. Now that the vocation of women to the priesthood is recognised and acknowledged by the church, such women no longer feel that they have to apologise either for being women or for being priests. This is a liberating experience which allows the women to explore further what it means to be a woman who is a priest.

In the early years of the debate there were those who questioned whether women could actually do the job required of a priest. If this perception were to be challenged, the women had to work in a way similar to that of their male colleagues as the only way of exercising priesthood known in the Church of England at that time was the male pattern. Thus women began to show that they could actually do the job. With hindsight we realise that this approach raises many theological issues about ordination but for many it was a significant factor at the time. The point has now been proved, and for the past ten years or so there has been no debate about whether women could fulfil the functional role of priests. The result is now a freedom to explore other ways of exercising priesthood. No longer are the women expected to fulfil the stereotype set by male priests.

Thus changing patterns of priesthood are likely to emerge as women grow in confidence as women and in their priesthood and bring with them a new and enriching dimension to this ministry. This in turn may enable men to be more true to themselves and also find new ways of being priests. New opportunities appropriate to the church as it serves in today's society are opening up with this development.

## New styles of leadership

There have always been a few women in leadership roles in the church. This has been true from the time of the New Testament when Priscilla, Phoebe and Lydia are among the women named, and it has been true in most churches down the ages. Now that the number of women in such roles is increasing within the Church of England, new styles of leadership may well emerge. This will probably be a more collaborative style, achieved by negotiation rather than in an authoritative way. This may in fact be nearer to the servant/leader model, taught and exemplified by Jesus and commended to his disciples:

> Jesus said . . . 'You know that those who are regarded as rulers of the Gentiles lord it over them, and their high officials exercise authority over them. Not so with you. Instead, whoever wants to become great among you must be your servant, and whoever wants to be first must be slave of all. For even the Son of Man did not come to be served, but to serve, and to give his life as a ransom for many.'[3]

It may be that this collaborative style is a feature of how many women exercise leadership. It is a matter of fact that until very recently the majority of stipendiary women ministers have served for some considerable time as curates or in other assistant roles and have therefore by definition been part of a leadership team in a church. It may be because of this experience that they have something to teach the church about team-work. The truth or otherwise of this will be seen as women become incumbents, team rectors, archdeacons, residentiary canons and deans of cathedrals. Cathedrals have often been criticised as places of discord among their senior staff; this may be because many deans, provosts and residentiary canons have been competent parish priests who did a very good job when in charge of a parish but are less able to work well with other similarly qualified clergymen. I wonder if the women will manage any better! We shall not know the answer to that question until we have cathedrals where there are at least two senior women clergy on the staff. Where a woman joins a fairly large team of men, such as is true of bishop's staff meetings and of cathedral chapters, she may have an important but limited influence. It will be when the proportion of women to men increases significantly that the style of leadership is likely to change in a marked way. What will be interesting also will be the effect when some of these clergy teams, including team ministries, are led by women. There is a danger that too much analysis will be directed towards the first few women in such positions. The limited value of such an analysis will be simply because with their colleagues these women will be still working out their own leadership style. It is also likely that there may not be a clearly defined way that all women will work. Some women will lead in ways very similar to many men and already we have some men who are very good at collaborative leadership. To what extent the women clergy will have changed leadership styles will be an interesting subject for study in ten or twenty years time.

## A new dimension in the councils and committees of the church

To date most of the diocesan and deanery councils and committees have had a predominantly male membership. Increasingly women clergy will take their place alongside laywomen. As the proportion of men to women changes and more women clergy are appointed to chair boards and councils, so the dynamics of these meetings will change.

As there will be a more varied pool of clergy upon which to call it is hoped that the best people, regardless of gender, will serve the church in this way. Within a parish church leadership team the presence of women can similarly change the feel and the agenda of a staff meeting. The intuitive gifts of women and the importance that they attach to relationships and feelings will affect how the staff team functions and the items that are considered important for discussion. The agenda may become less programme- and more people-orientated. Whether these will be changes for better or worse remains to be seen but changes there will be, to which all will have to adapt.

### *New gifts and insights*

The above changes can be summed up by saying that with the ordination of women to the priesthood, new gifts and insights will be at the service of the church from within the priesthood. This will encourage and complement the gifts and potential of the laity that are already being used for the extension of the kingdom of God.

### *Mission and evangelism*

That women are now included in the priesthood of the Church of England means that for many this church is now more credible and more likely to be taken seriously by women and men and not least by young professional women. No longer can the church be accused of being an 'exclusively male club' which has no place for women. Loyal church members have always known that the church is for all, but to those who are not church members this has not always been apparent. The ordination of women is not the whole answer but it does remove one obstacle that has prevented some from even considering the claims of Christ. It also means that the church can now make better use of its human resources rather than insisting that some of its woman-power be severely curtailed.

## Gender issues

The ordination of women has made gender issues in the church both more and less important. For those who cannot accept this development as consistent with the tradition of the church, true to biblical interpretation or helpful to ecumenical relationships, the matter of gender is now much more important. The presence of women in the sanctuary, pulpit or in positions of leadership is a matter of concern, debate and discrimination.

For those who see this as a movement of the Spirit of God and wholly consistent with developing tradition and biblical interpretation, the issue of gender is now less important. There is now the possibility that the appointment of clergy can be based on the qualities that are appropriate rather than on gender. To most people, gatherings of clergy which include both men and women feel more natural and are a reflection of the created order. The words from Genesis ring true, 'It is not good for the man to be alone'.[4]

Only time will tell whether the women clergy will have the same opportunities to exercise their gifts and experience as have their male colleagues. Indications from other parts of the Anglican Communion and from other denominations that already have women ministers, suggest that discrimination against the women may remain for many years to come. Will parishes that have a significant and challenging ministry be as open to women as to men incumbents or will most of the women clergy still be found in the small, downtown parishes? These may in fact be the very places where experienced ministers are needed and the women will no doubt do a good and faithful work in such places. The question is will the playing field be level for the women? Will they be integrated into the ordained ministry and be found at all levels of leadership in the church? In a few years' time will the women clergy experience the glass ceiling that many other professional women find in their careers? It may be true that clergy do not have a career but a vocation. If that is true it ought to be so for male and female clergy in the same way. Although women in the episcopate is not an issue explored in any depth in this book, it may prove to be an increasingly significant factor as the integration or otherwise of women clergy into the leadership of the church develops in the next few years. Gender issues for the church have certainly not all been solved by ordination of women to the priesthood.

## *Clergy marriages*

The ordination of women to the priesthood raises issues within the clergy family when the ordained partner is the woman. In one sense this is not new, as married women who were deacons and deaconesses, especially if they were in stipendiary ministry, had to work out their role, as did their husbands also. However, this issue, like many others, has been highlighted now that women are priests. The Church of England sets great store by its married priesthood. There has been a traditional and important role for the vicar's wife and many parishes like to have 'children in the vicarage'. Should the clergy wife wish to remain a layperson but feel called to work closely with her husband in his ministry such a partnership is given and received as a gift to the church. Yet this traditional husband and wife team as a feature of Church of England ministry is much less common than it was a generation ago. The role of the vicar's wife has been changing as more clergy wives have their own career and are no longer available for the considerable amount of pastoral work that was often undertaken by their predecessors.

The role of the clergy husband however has no tradition attached to it. In British society it is still, to a large extent, expected that the husband's career or employment will take precedence over that of his wife and so it is expected that the clergy husband will have his own career and the ordained wife will fit her ministry around her husband's work. This is one of the reasons for such a high proportion of ordained women being honorary clergy. The church and society will have to adjust to the idea that when the ordained partner is the woman the husband will need to be as supportive of his wife's vocation as is the vicar's wife of her husband's vocation. The husband may need to be prepared to move into the parsonage house and possibly give up or relocate his employment. Unlike the case of the clergy wife, it is not expected that the clergy husband will be the unpaid curate, although if he feels called to be available in a parish as the traditional vicar's wife has been, then that also ought to be seen as a gift to the church. The role of the clergy husband has yet to be developed. Perhaps he will be able to help the church work out a new role and possibly abandon a stereotype role for the clergy spouse.

Another issue arises when both husband and wife are ordained. When research was carried out for the report 'Deacons Now' in 1990 there were 159 couples where both partners were ordained, which represented 16% of the women who were deacons. The number of such couples has undoubtedly grown since then. Since women have been priested this issue has also become more significant because of sacramental and employment factors. When the wife is a priest she will not only have her professional role within the parish where she may remain as the curate, whether stipendiary or honorary, but liturgically she will now no longer function exclusively as a deacon but from time to time will preside at the eucharist. For many women, especially those who are wives and mothers, this often feels quite natural. At home she is used to preparing meals and feeding the family; now at the Lord's table she is doing something similar at a sacramental level. When a parish is fortunate to have both a man and a woman priest on the staff, there is a wholeness about their ministry, representing the wholeness of humanity and the wholeness of God in whose image both man and woman are created. When both partners in a marriage are ordained, especially if the marriage is a strong one, then important but new images of being 'one in Christ Jesus'[5] are being enacted. The church has yet to understand fully the significance of this new phenomenon.

On the practical level the church, in many dioceses, is still unclear about how to employ the priest who is a woman if she is married to a priest. Such women are now eligible to be incumbents. The church as well as the couple themselves have to work out how best to use this resource. Different ways of deploying such couples are emerging. Sometimes it is in the traditional role of the husband holding the incumbency. Some couples decide to take it in turns to seek the stipendiary post while the partner remains honorary if a second stipendiary post is not available. Sometimes one will take an incumbency and the other seek a sector ministry, or a couple may move to a united benefice with each having responsibility for one or more of the churches in the benefice. This may give job satisfaction, but may only carry one stipend so that the couple are financially disadvantaged. There are always questions to be asked about the relative value of two ministers who are married to each other working in the same or in different parishes. The resident parson has a valued place in the parochial system. If both partners were to be incumbents, this feature would be lost for one of the parishes concerned. The Church of England has to think through the importance of residence for all clergy. The principle is being eroded as benefices are united and already in many rural areas the vicar lives in one of the neighbouring villages.

It is becoming obvious that the ordination of women to the priesthood is challenging some traditional patterns of vicarage life. This ought not to be seen as a threat but as a new and significant resource available to the church. How best to use this resource and its effect upon the shape of the Church of England is but one more challenge that has been highlighted by this development in the priesthood.

*Inclusive language*

The demand for inclusive language in the context of worship, especially when referring to people, has been growing over the years. Although not initiated by the ordination of women, undoubtedly it is highlighted as women take a more prominent role in leading worship. No longer are male generic words acceptable to many laity and clergy. For example when the priest leading people in public confession is a woman, it feels incongruous to be using the words of the Alternative Service Book and so to be encouraging the congregation to 'live in love and peace with all men' and to confess that, 'we have sinned . . . against our fellow men'. A visitor to a church might think that Christians believe that only men cause discord and that we only need to confess the sins that we have committed against the male of the species. This is obviously not the case and not what the words mean. It is because of the exclusive language of current liturgy that there are likely to be further changes in the language of worship to make it more consistent in meaning with other patterns of speech. As the Alternative Service Book is revised for the year 2000 such changes in liturgy can be expected.

More controversial is the use of exclusively male names, pronouns and metaphors for the almighty triune God. We are likely to see a demand for a more comprehensive use of word pictures found in the scriptures to describe God, including the feminine images. An example of this comes from Jesus who likened himself to a 'hen gathering her chicks'.[6] A study of scripture also reveals that the feminine pronoun is often used for the Holy Spirit and this may find its way into some of our liturgies. It would be unfortunate and equally unscriptural if there were a trend to replace all masculine words with feminine ones, but the use of images drawn from both male and female attributes would give a more balanced understanding of the character of God as well as being more consistent with the range of scriptural images.

Moses speaks of his pastoral care for the Israelites 'as a nurse cares for an infant',[7] and Paul writes that his care of the Thessalonians was 'like a mother caring for her little children'.[8] If this picture language to describe the pastor/priest caring for his flock is appropriate for the men who are pastors, how much more so is it appropriate for women pastors.

The scriptures provide us with a rich source of images to describe God and the care of his people. The ordination of women may remind us of this rich resource and encourage us to draw from it more deeply than at present.

## The unity of the church

Paradoxically, the inclusion of women in the priesthood of the Church of England has resulted in a greater sense both of unity and of division. The latter is more obvious, as many of those who believe this to be a wrong or retrograde step no longer feel able to receive the sacrament from the hands of some of the priests of their own church or in some cases even to be in the presence of a woman priest or with those who agree with such a development. For laypeople who cannot receive from a priest who is a woman there is always the fear that such a priest will be celebrating should they visit another church. 'We are now a divided church', feels very true in some places and this is regrettable. There are those who believe that relationships with the Roman Catholic and Orthodox Churches have been hindered even though the Church of England is only a small part of the Anglican Communion. Over this issue the Church of England has lost and gained membership including some fine clergy. The only statistics that are kept are those for the numbers of clergy who resign over this issue: 209 clergy resigned in 1994.

However, for those who believe this to be of God, there is relief that the debates and arguments that polarised people and absorbed so much time are now over and the church can get on with its mission. Many who before the decision were uneasy about this development, have now accepted it as the mind of the church and are learning to live with and even appreciate the contribution that women are bringing to the priesthood. It has also brought the Church of England in line with a growing number of Anglican provinces and with other denominations who have already taken this step.

The legislation that allowed women to be ordained to the priesthood also included what have been called conscience clauses. These enable a parish to declare that it will not permit a woman to preside at a communion service and/or will not accept a woman as the next incumbent. The reason for this inclusion in the legislation is to respect the consciences of those who cannot accept the ordination of women to the priesthood. The Church of England has declared that such people shall retain a respected place within its ranks. One of the results is that built into the present structures of this church is an agreement to differ over the issue. At one level this can be seen as a positive attempt to live with our differences, and sets a good example. At another level it means that discrimination against women who are priests is now part of our structures. This is a tension that attempts to respect what are called 'the two integrities'. It will be interesting to see for how long the Church of England can live with this tension.

Another issue of which we have become more aware since this decision of the Church of England has been the pressure groups in the Roman Catholic Church in England for women to be ordained as Roman Catholic priests. On a personal note I remember that at the ordinations in Rochester Cathedral in May 1994 the only demonstration outside the cathedral on that occasion was by those campaigning for women to be admitted to the Roman Catholic priesthood.

### Correction to a mistaken theology about God

The debate over the ordination of women raised many issues including our understanding of God. It was alarming to discover that the debate revealed that many people believed God to be male in gender. This was probably reinforced by the fact that all priests were men and by the exclusive language of our liturgy. The English language is limited. If neither male nor female pronouns are used to describe God, the result is an impression of a God who is impersonal, which is not in line with the image of God as revealed in the scriptures. Orthodox Christian belief, while recognising the historical truth of the maleness of Jesus, has understood the almighty triune God to be beyond gender. The ordination of women may help to redress this misunderstanding, not to lead to the belief in God as female but to return to the belief expressed in the Thirty-nine Articles, of a God 'without body, parts or passions' (Article 1).

## *The humanity of Jesus*

Also at a theological level the debate in question revealed an inadequate theology of the incarnation in that some believed that the maleness of Jesus took priority over his humanity. While it is historically true that Jesus was male, the orthodox position is that he became human. The words, 'was made man', that appear in the Nicene Creed, mean that he was made human, not just a male. This is something that the Cappadocian Fathers would surely have stressed. When they were dealing with heresy concerning the true humanity of Jesus, they coined the phrase, 'What he did not become he could not redeem'. In this present context that would mean that although his humanity was expressed in the male form, the incarnation was about God becoming human and in some way embracing both sexes. If he only became a male then he is the saviour of males only. For women it is vitally important that he became human. Their very salvation depends upon it.

## Conclusion

The ordination of women has meant changes in the Church of England. For some it is a change for the better, for others a retrograde step. Most of us find change difficult. The familiar feels safe and thus this change along with all the other changes that are taking place at present make the church feel a less safe place. Yet change is inevitable if the church is to be true to its mission. Such change must not be for its own sake but in order that the church may be obedient to the leading of the Spirit of God and true to its mission of proclaiming and living the unchanging gospel in a changing society. May the ordination of women to the priesthood equip the church to be more effective in the mission to which God has called her.

## Notes

Biblical quotations are all from the New International Version.

1 John 15.5.
2 1 Corinthians 12.27.
3 Mark 10.42–5.
4 Genesis 2.18.
5 Galatians 3.28.
6 Matthew 23.37.
7 Numbers 11.12.
8 I Thessalonians 2.7.